cooking *for* two

cooking

for two

---

120 Recipes for Every Day and Those Special Nights

Bruce Weinstein and Mark Scarbrough

WM

WILLIAM MORROW

An Imprint of HarperCollins Publishers

To Susan Ginsburg,
career cartographer, patient yea-sayer,
and friend

HarperCollins books may be purchased for educational, business, or sales promotional use. For information please write: Special Markets Department, HarperCollins Publishers Inc., 10 East 53rd Street, New York, NY 10022.

FIRST EDITION

Designed by Nicola Ferguson

Printed on acid-free paper

Library of Congress Cataloging-in-Publication Data
Weinstein, Bruce, 1960–
    Cooking for two / Bruce Weinstein and Mark Scarbrough.
      p. cm.
    ISBN 0-06-052259-3 (hc. : alk. paper)
    1. Cookery for two.   I. Scarbrough, Mark.   II. Title.

TX652.W383   2004
641.5'61—dc21

                        2003045867

08 WBC/QW 10 9 8 7 6

Contents

Acknowledgments

Two in the kitchen perhaps, but many elsewhere.

We'd like to thank Harriet Bell—more than our editor, no less than our friend. She inspired this book, continues to goad us to do the best work, has the best eye for what works, and remains the savviest person we know in the food world.

At HarperCollins, our gratitude to Carrie Bachman and Gypsy Lovett, the dynamic duo of marketing. Roberto de Vicq de Cumptich continues to have an amazing eye for design; Ann Cahn manages to make making books easy (clearly a miracle worker, she). Ginger McRae is a whiz with the details—she must be a saint, given that we hear God lives in there as well. Mary Speaker has designed all our books with an impeccable eye; this time, Nicola Ferguson crafted a beauty for us. Jessica Peskay has gracefully—no, blessedly—overseen the production; Katie Connery has kept it all moving along nicely—no small task in a world of so many competing agendas.

We'd be remiss not to thank Annie Leuenberger for her encouragement and laughter. She's now sadly left the city for that brighter shore always looming on the horizon: California.

Outside publishing, we'd like to thank Robert Steinberg at Scharffen Berger Chocolate Maker for his ongoing support. Lee Wooding at Cuisinart provided us with a mini food processor that got a real workout testing these recipes. And could we ever say enough about Amy Kull at Fleischman Hillard for her outright support?

Toques off to David Weinstein and Lisa Aiello at Vox Advertising and Design for cultivating our web site over the years. Beth Shepard continues to make sure we're plucking out a tune on the national marketing bandwagon. And finally, Marianne Macy. She's so often eaten pasta at ten in the morning and listened to our gripes—and then taken home the leftovers. Who else would return with typed notes on the dishes the next day?

Introduction

Remember the old song "Tea for Two"? Romantic, yes—but hardly the stuff of most cookbooks, which offer recipes for what happens long after you've had your tea for two: once the kids come along, once the company starts dropping by. Sautés for six, casseroles for eight, cakes for ten.

We've come by these grand designs honestly enough. Consider the holidays. Thanksgiving dinner may be the single most important meal of the year—and that's not to mention Hanukkah, Christmas, or even the traditional Fourth of July picnic. The crowded cooking spirit of those celebrations surely works itself back into our notions of everyday cooking. So we're left with a 9 × 13-inch casserole on an ordinary Thursday night.

And what about the images we've seen on TV? *The Brady Bunch, The Waltons,* or even *My Three Sons?* Most of us would say the average American family has a mom, a dad, and two kids, if not more. But the

U.S. Census Bureau reported in 2000 that the average U.S. family had just 3.14 members; the average household, just 2.59 members.

So despite our 9 × 13 dreams, we cook in smaller pots. And even if we occasionally cook for crowds, we get to those celebrations the old-fashioned way: by starting out with just two. We date, fall in love, get married. Or perhaps it's not even as romantic as that. We have a standing dinner date with a friend on Wednesday nights, just the two of us.

We also tend to end up as twosomes: the children off to college, or on their own. Perhaps we lose a spouse. Or start over, a new life. Dating at forty, fifty, sixty. Or even this: the kids go away for the weekend, a week, or the summer, off to the grandparents or sports camp. So what do you do with that cherished meatloaf recipe? Make it and you're stuck with leftovers for a week. And cookies? One batch, four dozen.

So here's a cookbook for smaller pots. For mac and cheese, that comforting weeknight supper, but this time without any leftovers or any waste. Or for peanut butter oatmeal cookies. Six is the perfect number on Saturday night after the movies.

cooking in small batches without that half-a-can-of-stock predicament

If you've ever cooked a typical recipe for two, you know the shtick. You use half a can of stock, or less, and then what? You're left with that irritating can in the refrigerator, the one with aluminum foil wadded across the top, the one you throw out a week later. And what happens when the recipe calls for, say, two teaspoons of chopped onion? A week later, you come across those wiggly, brown slivers, laminated in plastic wrap, turning to mulch in your crisper.

We decided part of the secret to successful small-batch cooking was doing it without waste. So we've crafted techniques to cut down on the yield without larding your refrigerator with leftover bits and pieces. *You'll buy what you use, use what you buy.* For example, a small chicken egg is too large for a batch of six cookies or two brownies; so we offer alternatives: either pasteurized egg substitutes such as Egg Beaters or quail eggs. Instead of half a can of stock, we use the liquid that dried mushrooms have soaked in, or we make a small amount of broth with vegetables and herbs before adding meat to the stew. We use shallots instead of onions, vermouth (which keeps for months) instead of wine (which sometimes turns within hours of opening), and dried spices instead of fresh whenever appropriate.

Unfortunately, buying just what you'll use isn't always so easy. At first glance, the modern supermarket is of little help. These days, everything is super-sized; tomatoes and onions have swollen to terrifying proportions.

But our big supermarkets can actually be quite helpful. Many now have butcher counters that will sell you one or two chicken breasts, or a quarter pound of hamburger; many sell grains or spices in bulk, allowing you to measure out what you need. At gourmet markets—and some neighborhood supermarkets that are getting in on this act—you can now buy a sprig of rosemary or a handful of mushrooms. Beets are in tubs; tomatoes, in baskets. True, you may have to dig for the petite versions under their gargantuan kin, but they're down there. If not, let the produce manager of your market know there are people like you looking for smaller-sized bags of things like potatoes.

In our recipes, there are two notable exceptions to the "buy what you use" rule. First: dairy products. There are quantities in the ingredient lists such as "2 tablespoons heavy cream." There was simply no way to make a two-serving cream soup using a whole carton of cream—not without creating what could only be described as a soup milk shake. We experimented with powdered cream, but it turned gummy in soups. Besides, it's not readily available. So up front, we admit we created recipes that used less than the whole when it comes to dairy. That said, cream is such a treat in your coffee the next morning!

The second exception is dried spices, various pantry staples, and the like. Of course, you can't buy the exact amount of, say, the flour you need for a recipe. Nonetheless, if stored properly, pantry staples will last for months, so buying a little now pays off the next time you cook.

fish and casseroles smell after three days

Pet peeve number one: making a big pot of stew and then having to resort to strategies like eating it for three days running, or dividing it into small batches that get shoved to the back of the freezer, then pitched six months later. So the economics of cooking for two is *not only to buy what you'll use, but also to make what you'll eat.*

For workday dinners in minutes, how about a pasta dish such as Ziti with Curry Carrot Cream Sauce that makes just enough for two without leftovers? For dinner on a cold Sunday night, try one of the three stuffed baked potato recipes, each individual casseroles that bake up light and very comforting, a winter warmer in two potato skins. For a summery salad that makes just enough so you don't have to get up from the deck and put things in the refrigerator when the fireflies come out, there's Southwestern Chicken Salad or fresh Seafood Salad.

There are also plenty of small-batch baking recipes: cookies, cakes, and cobblers. You can indulge tonight without indulging all week. And there are a few things fit for quiet celebrations, the kind two people can have: Crawfish Stuffed Artichokes and Lemon Meringue Tarts.

Tea for two. It wasn't such a bad idea after all.

Before You
Start Cooking

Most equipment for small-batch baking is a matter of common sense—use a small whisk, not a big balloon, to beat one egg and a teaspoon of sugar. But some pieces of equipment are necessary for precision's sake.

Baking Dishes Use a baking dish that's exactly the volume indicated. Smaller sizes mean volume variations are proportionally more momentous. Using a 3-cup instead of a 2-cup ramekin is like using a 9 × 13-inch baking dish instead of a 9-inch square.

If a savory recipe calls for a *1-quart round soufflé dish,* use a 1-quart baking dish with sides at least 3 inches high. When a recipe calls for a *shallow 1-quart casserole dish,* use the standard 1-quart variety, most likely square, with sides about 1½ inches high. In truth, with the exception of the Crab Saffron Soufflé, all the savory casseroles will work in either baking dish because the volumes are identical. The baking times, however, will be different. If you use a shallower dish than the recipe calls for, reduce the baking time by 10 percent or so, because more surface area is exposed to the heat. If you use a deeper dish than the recipe calls for, increase the baking time by 10 percent or so. (The result will also be gummier, less crusty.)

Cakes and other sweets are a tad less forgiving. The measurements and size (not just the volume) of the baking dish matters because of the more delicate balancing act sugar, fat, and protein perform as they interact in the oven.

Ceramic Ramekins   These are essential for some small cakes, brownies, and puddings. The recipes call for specific sizes—it's important not to make substitutions unless indicated in the recipe. All this back and forth about size and volume may seem schoolmarmish or, at worst, off-putting. But the point is merely to cook accurately in small batches because the proportions among ingredients are tighter.

Hand Mixer or Whisk   Most of these recipes that require beating work with either a whisk or an electric hand mixer. One egg yolk and 2 tablespoons of sugar don't even make it up to the beaters of most standing mixers.

Kitchen Scales   With an accurate scale, preferably a digital model that is accurate to ¼ ounce, you can weigh nuts, chocolate, vegetables, or meat to determine exactly how much you need.

Measuring Spoons   Because the recipes often call for ¼ or even ⅛ teaspoon of spices or leavenings, invest in measuring spoons that can accurately gauge these minuscule amounts. All measurements in this book are for level teaspoonfuls, tablespoonfuls, and cupfuls.

Mini Food Processor   A mini food processor is not required for the recipes in this book, but it's quite helpful. While not equipped with fancy gadgetry like a 1 mm slicing blade, it can finesse smaller amounts than a larger model, where, for example, the cutting blade simply passes over a teaspoon of parsley.

Paper Pastry Shells   Some baking recipes offer you the option of paper pastry shells. Long a professional baker's tool, these shells are now available to home bakers through baking supply stores and well-stocked gourmet markets. For the recipes in this book, use paper pastry shells that are 4 inches in diameter. One caveat: watch the baking time carefully. Made of paper, the shells don't cook as quickly as metal tins; you may need to increase the baking time by 10 or even 20 percent. For baking, they must be placed on a baking sheet, preferably an insulated one.

Saucepans and Skillets   As a rule of thumb, a small saucepan is 1 or 1½ quarts; a medium, 2 or 2½ quarts. A small skillet or sauté pan is 6 or 7 inches in diameter; a medium, 8 to 10 inches.

Springform Pans   One alternative to baking in a ramekin or a paper pastry shell is a small springform pan. Choose a 4-inch pan with a sturdy locking mechanism. A nonstick pan works best, but it can scratch if you use a knife or metal spatula to release the cake from the pan's bottom. If you use nonstick pans, use cookware specifically designed for this surface, such as heat-safe rubber spatulas and knives.

a quick reference guide to some ingredients

In the past, small-batch recipes suffered from lackluster flavors because the ingredients were pared down to the basics. To heighten the flavors in our recipes, we've called for a few ingredients that might not be familiar to you. Others such as onions and celery, less exotic but nonetheless in this list, might require a little explanation about purchasing and storing for small-batch cooking.

Ancho Chiles One form of dried poblano peppers (the other, mulatos, are smokier in taste), anchos are among the most aromatic dried chiles you can find. Look for whole, red, shiny, flexible anchos, without torn skins. They're available at most supermarkets (usually in the produce section), at all Latin American and Mexican markets, and from sources listed in the Source Guide (page 269).

Celery Since it cannot be bought one rib at a time, leave extra celery ribs attached to the root and store them in a sealed plastic bag in the hydrator for up to 2 weeks. If the ribs have gone limp, give them a fresh cut about one inch above the root end, then try refreshing them in a bowl of ice water for an hour. You may also find celery on the buffet at your neighborhood deli, supermarket salad bar, or take-out eatery. The quality, of course, varies dramatically, but you can always buy just what you need. In fact, supermarket salad bars can be a great resource when cooking in small batches: two small carrots, one radish, a single celery rib.

Chili Powder Chili powder is a blend of powdered dried chiles (often dried ancho chiles), dried oregano, and ground cumin; Mexican or Latin American brands can also include ground cloves, cinnamon, garlic, salt, and cilantro. Because of the chemical reaction among the spices' oils, chili powder goes stale quickly; store it in a cool, dark place for no more than three months.

Clam Juice Available bottled in most supermarkets, this is the liquid left over when clams are cooked. Buy it only in clear bottles; look for a pale white liquid, not beige or brown, with no sandy sediment.

Coconut Milk This thickened coconut liquid is made by simmering coconut meat in water, then straining the mixture. Do not substitute "cream of coconut," which is a sweetened coconut mixture made for desserts and tiki-bar drinks.

Dried Mushrooms Many of these recipes call for dried mushrooms, which are then reconstituted in hot water. Do not substitute fresh mushrooms when a recipe calls for dried. Buy dried mushrooms in clear packages; look for mushrooms that are whole and have a color similar to their fresh counterparts. Do not buy dried mushrooms that have been pounded to dust or that have turned gray from improper storage.

Eggs For much of the baking, we've used either quail eggs or pasteurized egg substitutes, such as Egg Beaters. Do not replace them with pasteurized egg whites, which lack a modified food starch that stabilizes baked goods.

Some recipes call for a whole egg, usually a medium egg, or just an egg white or a yolk. Egg whites and yolks can be stored in the refrigerator, tightly covered, for 2 days, to be added to scrambled eggs or omelets. Egg whites can also be frozen for up to 6 months. To freeze egg yolks, whisk a pinch of salt into each yolk to prevent coagulation, then freeze tightly covered for up to 3 months.

Herbs and Spices We've almost always given you the choice of using dried or fresh herbs. While we prefer fresh, the amounts called for are so small that they can cause leftover fresh herbs, so dried herbs are usually an alternative. In a few cases, we've called only for fresh herbs—usually because the dish cooks so quickly that dried herbs don't have time to soften. Dried herbs and spices can be kept in a cool, dark place for up to 6 months. Ground spices, such as mustard or cinnamon, have a slightly longer shelf life. Dried leafy spices take on a tealike taste when stale.

Liquid Smoke It can cause fights in some parts of the country among purists, but liquid smoke is an easy way to get a smoky flavor into casseroles. Still, it's optional in all our recipes. Despite one brand eponymously so-named, there are many varieties, usually made with mesquite or hickory. The best are simply wood smoke distillate and water, not cut with stabilizers or artificial flavorings.

Mango Chutney Every supermarket carries Major Grey's, one version of this vinegary, jamlike sauce made from mangoes and spices. But it's a pale imitation compared to what's available in some gourmet markets, at East Indian markets, or from outlets listed in the Source Guide (page 269).

Nam Pla Nam pla imparts the characteristic taste to many Thai dishes—so much so that this fermented mixture of fish and spices is often called the soy sauce of Southeast Asia. Quite pungent, the flavors mellow beautifully when heated. Its slightly milder Vietnamese cousin, nuoc mam, can be substituted.

Nuts Store them, shelled or not, in the freezer in sealed plastic bags or other airtight containers; there, they will stay fresh for about a year. They can be tossed directly from the freezer into a dry skillet for toasting; otherwise, let them come to room temperature before using them in a recipe.

Onions For these recipes, a "small onion" is 2 to 2½ inches in diameter. Pre-chopped onions are available in the freezer section of some supermarkets. While the quality of this frozen convenience varies dramatically, it can be a time saver in a pinch.

Pancetta This cured Italian bacon is not smoked. Pressed into a roll, it's usually available at the butcher counter or some deli counters. Have the butcher slice off a piece just the size you need. If you buy extra, store it tightly wrapped in the freezer for up to 4 months.

Paprika Paprika is made from ground red peppers; it's usually labeled "mild" or "hot." All the recipes in this book were made with mild paprika. If you prefer a dish with far more heat, try the hot, sometimes labeled "hot Hungarian paprika." Because of the interaction of the chile oils, paprika loses its power soon after the container is opened. Store it in a cool, dry, dark place for no more than three months. If yours is bordering on stale, you might be able to refresh it by heating it in a dry skillet over very low heat for about 2 minutes, or until fragrant.

Parmigiano-Reggiano This aged skimmed-milk cheese from Italy has no substitute. There are some American brands, but they have a less complex taste, as well as a bit more tang. Buy Parmigiano-Reggiano in chunks from a large wheel with the name of the cheese stamped on the rind (a sign of authenticity).

Peanut Oil American peanut oils tend to be mild; Chinese bottlings smell and taste more like peanuts. A necessity for many Southern, Cajun, and Chinese dishes, peanut oil can go rancid—always smell it before using. Store it tightly covered in the refrigerator for up to 6 months. Some bottlings may cloud and solidify in the refrigerator—let the oil reliquefy and come back to room temperature before using.

Pepitás These pale green pumpkin seeds are common in Mexican and southwestern cooking. You can find them in most health food stores, at some gourmet stores, or from outlets listed in the Source Guide (page 269). They are sold salted or unsalted, hulled or still in their shell. The recipes in this book call only for unsalted, hulled pepitás.

Potatoes When buying potatoes in bulk, do not store them in your refrigerator; at 40°F, potato starch begins to break down within fifteen minutes. Store potatoes in a cool, dark place, but not with the onions and shallots, the fumes of which will encourage the potatoes to sprout.

Quail Eggs Even when baking in small batches, egg proteins are still necessary for making cookies and cakes. The perfect-sized answer? Quail eggs, which have begun showing up in many markets.

Because the shells are slightly gelatinous, quail eggs can be difficult to crack. To do so, use a sharp paring knife to saw off a small bit of the top; with your finger or a tiny spoon, scoop out the tiny white and yolk.

If you can't find quail eggs, use pasteurized egg substitutes, such as Egg Beaters, as an alternative; these can be precisely measured out. We have not called for small chicken eggs because these are not readily available. Indeed, it is illegal to sell them in some locales. Besides, a small chicken egg is still too much egg for some of these recipes.

Red Chili Paste A mixture of dried chiles, fermented beans, garlic, and thickeners, this Chinese condiment is also sold under names such as "chili paste with garlic" or "Szechwan chili sauce," or under brand names such as Lan Chi or Sun Wah. You can find it in the Asian aisle of most large supermarkets or in all Asian grocery stores. Quite fiery, it should be used sparingly if you have concerns about the heat of the dish. Store red chili paste in the refrigerator for up to 2 years. If you can't find red chili paste, substitute an equivalent amount of a mixture of equal parts red pepper flakes and canola or other vegetable oil—although the taste will be less aromatic, less complex, and more biting.

Rice Vinegar Made from fermented rice and sorghum, rice vinegar is one of the oldest condiments in Asian cooking. Although it comes in many colors and flavors, some quite pungent, all the recipes in this book use white (or clear) unseasoned rice vinegar, the mildest version, available in the Asian section of many supermarkets and in all Asian markets. In a pinch, substitute apple cider vinegar.

Saffron Threads Long the world's most treasured spice, saffron is sold in minuscule amounts, a few threads (or stigmas from a variety of purple crocus) per package. It's often available at the manager's desk in supermarkets. Look for whole, brightly colored threads, whether red or yellow; they should not be powdered. Store any unused threads in a small, airtight container in a dark, cool place for up to 8 months.

Shallots Shallots taste like a cross between an onion and garlic, but they look like garlic, with papery hulls and individual cloves, usually two per head. Recipes in this book refer to the entire shallot, all the cloves together. Remove the papery hull, then chop the cloves as you would an onion. Do not refrigerate shallots; store them in a dark, cool place for up to a month. If they sprout, they have lost their usefulness.

Shao Shing A Chinese rice wine made from glutinous rice, Shao Shing is used to flavor many Asian dishes. In some bottlings, it's labeled "Shaoxing" or "Hua Tiao" (that is, "carved flower," because of the carvings on the urns in which it is aged). Stored in a cool place, it can be kept for up to two years. Substitute dry sherry in a pinch—but never substitute Japanese sake or rice vinegar.

Shrimp All monikers used for shrimp—"jumbo," "large," or "colossal"—are mere window-dressing; they carry no official imprimatur. It's best to buy shrimp according to how many make up a pound; 30 to 35 per pound would be about average for "medium" shrimp. If you're squeamish about peeling and deveining them, have your fishmonger do this for you. Unless specifically called for, do not use precooked shrimp, sometimes sold as "cocktail shrimp."

Sugar Unless otherwise stated, "sugar" means granulated sugar. Light or dark brown sugar (the difference is the amount of molasses added to granulated sugar) should be packed into tablespoon and cup measures to remove any air between the grains.

Tomatillos Sometimes called Mexican green tomatoes, tomatillos are closely related to gooseberries. (You can tell because of their papery husks.) Purchase tomatillos that are bright green and, if possible, still have the husks attached. Tomatillos can be found in the produce section of most markets, often with the tomatoes, as well as in almost all Latin American markets.

Tomato Paste Until recently, tomato paste was available only in cans, a sticking point when you only need a tablespoon or two. Now it's widely available in squeeze tubes. Reseal the tube and store it in the refrigerator for up to 3 months.

Vermouth This is a great substitute for wine in small-batch cooking because you needn't worry about it going bad after you've used a small amount. Store vermouth at room temperature in a cool, dark place for up to a year. Our recipes call only for dry vermouth, sold with a white label. Do not substitute sweet red vermouth, a concoction best kept for cocktails, or the Italian aperitif Bianco, sometimes sold as vermouth.

the everyday pantry

A well-stocked pantry helps you avoid those there's-nothing-in-the-house-so-let's-go-out moments. In all cases, we have not hesitated to use small amounts of these items. That said, you needn't run out and buy this list before you start. It's just a handy guide to things that will keep for months on end, used in small portions in these recipes.

All-purpose flour, preferably
    unbleached
Baking powder, preferably
    double-acting
Baking soda
Black pepper
Brandy or Grand Marnier
Bulgur wheat
Canola or other vegetable oil
Chocolate
    bittersweet or dark squares or
        chips
    semisweet chips
    unsweetened squares or chips
Cocoa powder
Confectioners' sugar
Cornstarch
Cream of tartar
Dried bread crumbs
Dried fruit
Dried pastas
Frozen puff pastry
Garlic
Green peppercorns
Herbs and spices
    bay leaves
    caraway seeds
    cardamom pods
    celery seeds
    cinnamon sticks
    cloves
    crystallized ginger
    curry powder
    dried basil

dried cilantro
dried dill
dried oregano
dried parsley
dried rosemary
dried thyme
dry mustard
grated nutmeg
ground allspice
ground cinnamon
ground cloves
ground cumin
ground ginger
mild paprika
red pepper flakes
rubbed (ground) sage
sesame seeds
star anise pods
turmeric
Hoisin sauce
Honey, preferably an aromatic
    wildflower variety
Instant espresso powder
Jam
Ketchup
Maple syrup
Mayonnaise
Molasses, preferably
    unsulphured
Mustard, preferably smooth
    Dijon mustard
Nuts
    blanched almonds
    hazelnuts

pecans
pepitás
pine nuts
slivered almonds
unsalted cashews
unsalted peanuts
walnuts
Olive oil
Pastas
Peanut butter, preferably
smooth
Quinoa
Rice, white and jasmine
Rolled oats
Rum
Salt
Sesame oil
Solid vegetable
shortening

Soy sauce
Stock (beef, chicken, or
vegetable, preferably fat free
and no salt added)
Sugar (granulated and brown)
Tabasco sauce
Tapioca
Tofu, preferably brands such as
Mori-Nu, which require no
refrigeration
Unsalted butter
Vanilla extract
Vinegar
apple cider
balsamic
red wine
white wine
Worcestershire sauce
Yellow cornmeal

five tips for success

1. Read a recipe completely before you start cooking. Many have waste-saving steps—particularly, steps that use different parts of the same ingredient. It's important to know where you're headed, so you don't inadvertently throw out something you'll need later.

2. Avoid substitutions. While some are easy and marked in the book (cider vinegar for rice vinegar, for example), others are more complicated. What would you substitute, say, for unsweetened chocolate? In the end, don't make substitutions unless they are specifically given in the recipe. When you're cooking and baking in

small batches, the balance of flavors, leavenings, and proteins is slightly more precarious.

3. Measure meticulously. If you were making a traditional, three-tier, chocolate layer cake for ten, you might not level off the flour in one of the cup measures. Perhaps it wouldn't make a noticeable difference; you'd only be adding 2 or 3 percent more flour to the cake. But if you don't level off the one tablespoon of flour in our brownie recipe, you'll be adding as much as 30 percent more flour to the batter. That's enough to turn two fudgy brownies dry and tough.

If you're a cook who likes to double the garlic or ground black pepper in recipes, we suggest you refrain with these. Doubling would mean the dish would be overwhelmed with garlic or pepper. More is not necessarily better when you're cooking in small batches.

4. Don't use a double boiler to melt chocolate. Half an ounce of chocolate is too small an amount to melt in a double boiler; it will coat the pan and you'll never get it all out. Instead, place the chopped chocolate in a small bowl. Place the small bowl inside a larger bowl filled with about an inch of very hot water. (Do not let any of the water spill into the chocolate.) Keep stirring until the chocolate melts. Or melt the chocolate in a small bowl in the microwave set on high, stirring every 30 seconds, until half the chocolate melts; then remove it from the microwave and stir until all the chocolate is melted.

5. Treat the cooking times as guidelines, not laws. Ovens are temperamental: some run hot; others, hot in spots. The best advice we can give? Use the visual cues in the text—"until the edges are brown," "until fluffy and pale yellow"—and test a dish yourself to see if it's done to your satisfaction.

Short answer: a lot of things. It can indicate a quick and simple dish. Or a homey, comforting one, like a cheesy casserole. Or a streamlined version of a classic, designed to fit into a busy schedule.

We've used three symbols to help you decide how a dish fits into the "everyday" rubric—in other words, what day would be appropriate to make which dish. Of course, this system is less than accurate. On an ordinary Wednesday night, you might find yourself making something we label as fit for a quiet weekend celebration. But we hope these symbols give you a fast reference point for using the recipes.

 An easy dish: ready in minutes with minimal cooking.

 A workday dish that involves a little more cooking, or perhaps minimal cooking but a little more preparation time.

 A dish suitable for more leisurely cooking, for quiet celebrations or nights when you can enjoy a slower dinner.

Soups
and Stews

Step away from that kettle and get down a small saucepan—because what's more comforting than soup, even when you're cooking for two? Yes, these recipes begin with minuscule amounts—1 shallot, 1 teaspoon olive oil, ¼ teaspoon pepper—but none compromises taste. We've simplified the technique in jambalaya to make it a workday meal, morphed Yankee pot roast into a simple stew, and created a Thai-inspired one-pot vegetarian dinner. In all cases, the trick is to let the flavors meld in a slow simmer, just a bubble or two. With a little patience, you'll have the deep flavors of a larger pot's worth of stew, all in a two-serving package. It's enough to push the Dutch oven into your cupboard's recesses and put stews back in your weekly repertoire.

MUSHROOM BARLEY SOUP

makes 2 hearty servings

Mushroom barley soup is an American diner favorite—if ever made at home, then usually made for crowds. But there's no reason it can't be made for two—with a few substitutions. It's often made with lima beans for added body, but a whole can of limas is too much for two servings and dried beans take hours to soak. Our answer? Lentils, which give the soup a somewhat lighter but still earthy flavor. Use any mixture of fresh mushrooms you want; for a treat, add to the mix some exotic varieties such as hen of the wood, black trumpets, or porcini. Serve this soup with a salad of greens, toasted pecans, and cubed goat cheese, dressed in a light vinaigrette.

1 tablespoon olive oil

1 small onion, finely chopped

1 medium carrot, peeled and finely chopped

1 medium celery rib, finely chopped

6 ounces fresh mushrooms, such as cremini, brushed clean and thinly sliced

One 14½-ounce can beef stock (regular, low-fat, or nonfat, but preferably low-sodium)

1 cup water

1 small Italian plum tomato, roughly chopped

3 tablespoons barley (not quick-cooking)

2 tablespoons green lentils

1 bay leaf

2 teaspoons chopped fresh rosemary, or 1 teaspoon chopped dried rosemary

½ teaspoon salt, or to taste

½ teaspoon freshly ground black pepper

1. Heat a medium saucepan over medium heat. Swirl in the oil, then stir in the onion, carrot, and celery. Cook for about 3 minutes, or until the carrots have softened somewhat and the onion is fragrant, stirring frequently. Stir in the mushrooms and cook for 2 minutes, or just until their juices begin to make a sauce in the pan, stirring frequently.

2. Once the mushrooms have begun to release their liquid, stir in the stock, water, tomato, barley, lentils, bay leaf, and rosemary. Bring the mixture to a simmer, cover, reduce the heat to low, and simmer for 1 hour, or until the barley and lentils are quite tender, stirring occasionally to prevent the barley from sticking to the pan's bottom. Season with salt and pepper, discard the bay leaf, and serve immediately.

ESCAROLE, WHITE BEAN, and ROASTED GARLIC SOUP 💼

makes 2 servings

Lettuce soup? Well, not exactly. This is an Italian classic, a satisfying stew of tender white beans and wilted escarole, a green related to frisée or curly endive, but much sweeter, once only available in early summer but now in our markets year-round, thanks largely to Spanish farmers. Traditionally, this soup is thickened with egg yolks or cream—but a roasted garlic purée makes the broth light yet very aromatic. Since escarole can be sandy, wash it carefully before adding it to the saucepan.

3 large garlic cloves, left unpeeled

1 tablespoon olive oil

2 ounces pancetta (see page 10), finely chopped

1 small onion, finely chopped

1 small head escarole (about 12 ounces), cored, shredded, and washed, but not dried

One 14½-ounce can chicken stock (regular, low-fat, or nonfat, but preferably low-sodium)

1 teaspoon chopped fresh sage, or ¼ teaspoon rubbed sage

One 15-ounce can Great Northern beans, or other white beans, drained and rinsed

¼ cup freshly grated Parmigiano-Reggiano (about 1 ounce)

¼ teaspoon salt, or to taste

¼ teaspoon freshly ground black pepper

1. Preheat the oven to 400°F. Loosely wrap the garlic cloves in a small piece of aluminum foil. Bake for 40 minutes, or until quite soft and sweet-smelling. Open the packet and set aside to cool.

2. Heat a medium saucepan over medium heat. Swirl in the oil, add the pancetta, and sauté for 2 minutes, or until just browned and frizzled at the edges, stirring frequently. Toss in the onion and cook for 3 minutes, or until pale but very fragrant, stirring often.

3. Add the escarole and cook only for about 1 minute, just until the greens begin to wilt, tossing them occasionally with two wooden spoons or tongs. Stir in the stock and sage, then raise the heat to medium-high and bring the mixture to a simmer. Reserve ¼ cup of the beans in a small bowl; stir the remainder into the soup. Cover the saucepan, reduce the heat to low, and simmer for 20 minutes.

4. Meanwhile, squeeze the garlic pulp from its papery hulls into the bowl with the reserved beans. Discard the hulls. Mash the pulp and beans with a fork until smooth. Alternatively, place the reserved beans and the roasted garlic pulp in a mini food processor and pulse 5 or 6 times, or until smooth, scraping down the sides of the bowl as necessary.

5. After the soup has cooked for 20 minutes, stir a small amount of the soup broth (say, ¼ cup) into the bean-garlic purée, just to dissolve it, then stir this mixture back into the soup, along with the grated cheese. Stir just until the cheese melts, season with salt and pepper, and serve immediately.

Serving Suggestions

Top each bowl with 1 tablespoon chopped, pitted black olives, or a small amount of purchased caponata (Sicilian eggplant salad). Since both olives and caponata can be quite salty, reduce the amount of salt in the soup to ⅛ teaspoon, or none at all.

Place a toasted round of bread in each bowl before adding the soup. For a richer soup, drizzle each toasted round with extra-virgin olive oil before placing them in the bowls.

Crack 2 large eggs into small custard cups or teacups. After you swirl in the garlic purée, but before you add the cheese, slip the eggs into the soup. Cover and continue cooking over low heat for 3 minutes, or until the eggs are poached. Gently ladle the soup and one egg into each serving bowl, then top each bowl with half the cheese. Season with salt and pepper before serving.

CELERY ROOT AND ALMOND SOUP *with* ROASTED SHALLOTS 🍷🍷

makes **2 servings**

This is a creamy soup, based on a standard served in Parisian bistros, but thickened with ground almonds. It's a sumptuous soup because of the celery root (also called celeriac), a globular root from a variety of stalk celery, prized for its powerful celery taste with parsley overtones. Look for a celery root that is firm, compact, and spherical (the latter to make peeling it easier). A vegetable peeler will remove most of the leathery skin, but use a paring knife to cut out the deeper crevasses.

½ cup sliced blanched almonds
4 medium shallots, peeled
1½ tablespoons olive oil
1½ tablespoons unsalted butter
1 small onion, chopped
1½ tablespoons all-purpose flour
One 14½-ounce can chicken stock (regular, low-fat, or nonfat, but preferably low-sodium)

2 tablespoons dry vermouth or white wine
1 small celery root (about 12 ounces), peeled, then cut into a ½-inch dice
⅓ cup heavy cream
½ teaspoon salt, or to taste
½ teaspoon freshly ground white pepper, optional
¼ teaspoon grated nutmeg

1. Preheat the oven to 350°F. Place the almonds on a baking sheet and toast them for about 6 minutes, or until lightly browned, turning occasionally. Remove them from the oven, but maintain its temperature.

2. Place the shallots in a small baking dish; toss them with the oil. Bake for about 30 minutes, or until soft and caramelized, stirring occasionally. Set aside to cool.

3. Meanwhile, grind all but 2 tablespoons of the toasted almonds until powdery in a large spice grinder or a mini food processor. Set the sliced almonds and the almond powder aside separately.

4. Melt the butter in a medium saucepan set over low heat. Sprinkle the onion into the butter, stir to coat, and then cook for 3 minutes, or until pale and translucent, stirring frequently. Do not brown the onion pieces, to ensure that the final soup will remain creamy white. If the onion does begin to brown, reduce the heat even further, or remove the pan from the heat for a minute or so to cool it down. (If the onion browns, the final taste will not be affected—just the appearance.)

5. Sprinkle the flour evenly over the onion, then whisk to combine. Continue cooking and whisking for 20 seconds so that the flour loses its raw taste, but do not brown the flour. Whisk in the stock and wine, raise the heat to medium-high, bring the mixture to a simmer, and continue whisking over the heat for about 30 seconds, or until thickened. Slip the celery root into the soup, stir well, and bring the mixture back to a simmer. Cover, reduce the heat to low, and simmer for 30 minutes, or until the celery root is tender when pierced with a fork, stirring occasionally.

6. Pour the thick, aromatic soup into a large blender or a food processor fitted with the chopping blade. If using a mini food processor, you will need to work in batches. Pulse 8 or 9 times, until puréed, scraping down the bowl with a rubber spatula as necessary. Return the puréed soup to the saucepan set over low heat; whisk in the ground almonds, cream, salt, white pepper (if using), and the nutmeg. Cook and whisk for about 1 minute, just until heated through. Cover, remove from the heat, and let stand for 5 minutes to infuse the taste of the almonds into the soup. Meanwhile, roughly chop the shallots for a garnish.

7. Divide the soup between two bowls. Top each with half the chopped shallots and half the toasted almonds. Serve immediately.

FRESH PEA SOUP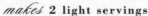

makes **2 light servings**

Because they show up in many markets in mid-May, or even earlier in parts of the South and West, fresh peas signal late spring. Or they're a harbinger of summer, ready and full just before the first heat wave, a blow that strikes them bland and shriveled. Here's an easy way to turn them into a light, tasty soup at their peak. Nonfat milk actually works best because the delicate taste of the peas is not overwhelmed by too much creaminess. Serve this soup warm or cold, depending on whether you've made it ahead—and the day's weather!

1 cup milk (regular, low-fat, or nonfat; see headnote)
2 pounds peas in their pods, shelled, pods washed and reserved (see Note)
1 small carrot, peeled and sliced
1 small onion, quartered
3 cups water
¼ teaspoon salt, or to taste
¼ teaspoon freshly ground black pepper

1. Bring the milk to a light boil in a small saucepan set over medium heat. Reduce the heat to low and simmer for about 4 minutes, or until reduced by half, stirring occasionally. Cover the pan and set aside off the heat.

2. Bring the pea pods (not the shelled peas), carrot, onion, and water to a boil in a medium saucepan set over high heat. Reduce the heat to low and simmer, uncovered, for 20 minutes.

3. Strain the vegetables and their light broth through a fine-mesh sieve, a chinoise, or a colander lined with cheesecloth, sit over a bowl. Discard the vegetable solids, return the broth to the saucepan, and set over medium-high heat. Bring the broth back to a simmer and cook for about 5 minutes, or until reduced to 1 cup. Add the shelled peas and cook for only 30 seconds, just until their color turns a shockingly bright green.

4. Pour the peas and the broth into a large blender or into a food processor fitted with the chopping blade. Purée in pulses until thick, scraping down the sides of the bowl as necessary with a rubber spatula. Now pour in the reduced milk and purée for about 20 seconds, or until smooth and bright green. Season with salt and pepper.

5. Serve warm, or pour the soup into a large bowl and refrigerate for 2 hours, or overnight, until chilled. (If refrigerating overnight, cover the bowl after 2 hours.)

> NOTE: Look for pods that are firm and bright green, with no blackened soft spots. Shell the peas by grasping the remnants of the stem, as if it were the tab of a zipper, and "zipping" it down the inside curve of the pod. Gently pry the pod open to release the peas inside.

Adding More

If desired, divide any of the following as toppings between the two bowls:

2 tablespoons sour cream (regular, low-fat, or nonfat)
2 tablespoons yogurt (regular, low-fat, or nonfat)
2 teaspoons chopped fresh basil
1 teaspoon chopped fresh mint
1 teaspoon fresh thyme
½ teaspoon finely grated lemon zest

Or make this soup into a heartier meal by dividing 2 tablespoons sour cream, crème fraîche, or plain yogurt between the bowls, then lay any of the following on top, dividing them between the bowls:

6 ounces lump crabmeat, picked over for shells and cartilage
½ pound precooked cocktail shrimp, peeled and deveined
½ pound steamed, sautéed, or grilled tofu, cut into ½-inch cubes

THAI-INSPIRED SQUASH, MUSHROOM, *and* BASIL STEW

makes **2 hearty servings**

The secret to most Thai stews is the mélange of coconut milk, brown sugar, nam pla, and yellow Thai curry paste, a prepared mixture of spices and oil. Some brands of yellow Thai curry paste are fiery yet so sweet as to be almost flowery; others are quite bland. We prefer the Mae Ploy brand. In any event, Thai bottlings do not include ghee, or clarified butter, as do Indian brands. Yellow Thai curry paste is available in the Asian section of many markets and almost all Asian supermarkets. Store it in the refrigerator for up to 6 months. Substitute red Thai curry paste if you want a hotter dish.

1 tablespoon peanut oil
1 small shallot, thinly sliced
1 small garlic clove, slivered
8 ounces cremini mushrooms, or white button mushrooms, cleaned and cut into quarters
1 tablespoon yellow Thai curry paste (see headnote)
One 5½-ounce can coconut milk
2 tablespoons nam pla (see page 10)

1 tablespoon packed light brown sugar
1 medium acorn squash (about 1½ pounds), peeled, seeded, and cut into ½-inch cubes (see Note)
1 small red bell pepper, cored, seeded, and cut into ½-inch strips
3 small scallions, cut into thirds
6 fresh basil leaves

1. Heat a medium pot over medium heat. Swirl in the peanut oil, then stir in the shallot and garlic. Cook for 1 minute, or just until barely softened, stirring frequently. Do not let the garlic brown—it should just soften slightly and sizzle at the edges. Add the mushrooms and cook for 2 minutes, or until they give off their liquid, stirring frequently. Then reduce the heat to low, and cook undisturbed for about 3 more minutes, until the mushroom liquid has been reduced to a glaze.

2. Raise the heat to medium again and melt the yellow curry paste into the stew by slowly stirring and cooking for about 10 seconds. Once the mixture is smooth and smells quite fiery, stir in the coconut milk, nam pla, and brown sugar, scraping up any browned bits on the bottom of the pan. Bring the soup to a simmer before stirring in the squash, bell pepper, scallions, and basil. Cover, reduce the heat to very low, and simmer for 25 minutes, or until the squash is fork-tender, stirring occasionally. Serve immediately.

> **NOTE:** A vegetable peeler won't do the job of peeling a tough acorn squash. The easiest way to do it is to cut the squash in half, scoop out the seeds, then lay the halves cut side down on a cutting board. Use a paring knife to peel off the skin in long arcs, starting at the top of each half-globe and following the natural curve of the squash. Any small bits remaining can be peeled off with a paring knife once the larger strips have been removed.

FISH AND POTATO CHOWDER

makes **2 servings**

There's really just one secret to making a comforting chowder: don't add too much cream. The point is to let the velvety fat in the cream carry the flavors, so just a touch will enhance them without masking them. In this version of the classic New England fish chowder, a yellow potato is sliced with a vegetable peeler into long, thin strips. The result? Easy potato noodles, which thicken the soup and make it quite luxurious.

1 tablespoon plus 1 teaspoon unsalted butter, at room temperature
1 small onion, finely chopped
1 cup milk (regular, low-fat, or nonfat)
One 8-ounce bottle clam juice (see page 8)
1 medium yellow-fleshed potato (about 6 ounces), such as Yukon Gold, peeled (see headnote)

1 bay leaf
1 teaspoon fresh thyme, or ½ teaspoon dried thyme
⅔ pound hake, cod, or flounder fillets, cut into ½-inch pieces (see Note)
¼ cup heavy cream
1½ tablespoons all-purpose flour
½ teaspoon salt, or to taste

1. Melt 1 tablespoon of the butter in a medium saucepan set over low heat. Sprinkle the onion over the butter, stir well, and cook for about 3 minutes, or until limp but golden, stirring frequently. For the traditional look of a white chowder, do not let the onion brown. Stir in the milk and clam juice, raise the heat to medium, and bring the mixture to a slow simmer.

2. Use a vegetable peeler to slice off paper-thin strips of the peeled potato, letting them fall directly into the soup; then stir in the bay leaf and thyme. Cover the pan, reduce the heat to low, and simmer for about 10 minutes, or until the potatoes are tender, stirring often to prevent sticking.

3. Add the fish and cook uncovered for 5 minutes, stirring frequently. The soup may just barely come back to a boil in the time allotted. Stir in the cream, raise the heat to medium, and bring the soup to a full simmer.

4. Meanwhile, make a paste out of the flour with the remaining 1 teaspoon softened butter by mashing them together with the back of a fork in a small bowl or tea cup. Once the soup is simmering, whisk in this butter mixture; continue cooking and whisking for about 1 minute, or until the soup thickens. Season with salt and serve immediately.

NOTE: Always ask to smell fish fillets before you buy them. They should smell fresh and clean, like the ocean on a spring morning, never like the tidal flats on a summer afternoon.

JAMBALAYA

makes 2 generous servings

While there's no bigger crowd-pleaser in Louisiana than jambalaya, a thick stew of ham hocks, shrimp, and rice, it's just as good when made in a small batch. Jambalaya begins with a roux (or thickener) of peanut oil and flour; cook the roux over low heat until it's deep maroon, whisking frequently to keep it from sticking and scorching. If you have peanut allergies, substitute a tablespoon of unsalted butter, but lower the heat so the butter doesn't burn while the roux toasts. Although jambalaya is traditionally an all-day dish, we've turned it into one fit for your workday repertoire by substituting purchased smoked ham for the hocks.

1 tablespoon peanut oil (see headnote)

1½ tablespoons all-purpose flour

1 small onion, chopped

1 small cubanel pepper, seeded, cored, and chopped (see Notes)

1 medium celery rib, chopped

1 large garlic clove, minced

1 cup chopped smoked ham (about 5 ounces; see Notes)

One 14½-ounce can diced tomatoes

¼ cup white rice

2 teaspoons fresh thyme, or ¾ teaspoon dried thyme

⅛ to ¼ teaspoon cayenne pepper

8 medium (about 30 per pound) shrimp, peeled and deveined

1. Heat a medium saucepan over medium-high heat. Swirl in the oil, sprinkle the flour evenly over the oil, then immediately reduce the heat to very low. Cook undisturbed for 20 seconds, then whisk briefly to incorporate the flour into the oil. Now let the roux cook for one minute undisturbed, then cook for an additional 3 to 4 minutes, or until the mixture turns a deep reddish brown, whisking frequently.

2. Stir in the onion, pepper, celery, and garlic until they are coated with the roux—be careful: it's very hot and may splatter when it comes into contact with water on or in the vegetables. Raise the heat to medium and cook for 2 minutes, or until the vegetables soften considerably, but not until they're limp, stirring constantly. Add the chopped ham and cook for 2 minutes, stirring once or twice. Once the ham has begun to frizzle at the edges, stir in the tomatoes with their juice, the rice, thyme, and cayenne. Make sure the rice is completely submerged in the liquid; then cover, reduce the heat to low, and simmer for about 12 minutes, until the rice is tender. Stir once or twice while the stew is simmering to prevent any flour from falling out of suspension and sticking to the bottom of the pan. If it does, lower the heat even further, or remove the pan from the heat to slow down the cooking. In any case, stir the stew more frequently, but avoid pulling up any burned bits of flour on the pan's bottom.

3. Uncover the pan and stir in the shrimp. If the stew is too thick, stir in water in 1 tablespoon increments until it is again soupy but still thick. Cook, uncovered, for about 2 minutes, or until the shrimp are firm and pink, stirring once or twice. Serve immediately.

NOTES: A cubanel (sometimes spelled cubanelle, or called an Italian frying pepper) is a long, thin, green, fingerlike pepper, quite sweet and very aromatic. Substitute an Anaheim pepper or a small green bell pepper in a pinch.

Smoked ham is available in the deli case of most supermarkets. Ask the butcher to slice it quite thick, so the chopped pieces will not break down and melt in the stew. For a more authentic taste, buy a small smoked ham shank (a 10-ounce bone with meat) and cut the meat off yourself.

BOLIVIAN GREEN CHILE STEW 🧳

makes **2 hearty servings**

The warmed avocados give this spicy, homey stew from Bolivia a creamy richness; puréed garbanzo beans thicken it without excess fat. The mixture of sour cream and ground cumin isn't just a garnish for this dish—instead, it balances the flavors, adding a cool touch to this hearty, aromatic stew.

1 tablespoon canola or other vegetable oil

1 small onion, halved, then thinly sliced

1 small garlic clove, minced

½ pound pork stew meat, cut into 1-inch pieces

One 15-ounce can garbanzo beans (chickpeas), drained and rinsed

One 4-ounce can chopped green chiles (hot, medium, or mild), drained

One 14½-ounce can chicken stock (regular, low-fat, or nonfat, but preferably low-sodium)

1 small Hass avocado, peeled, pitted, and cut into ½-inch chunks

2 tablespoons chopped fresh cilantro, or 1 tablespoon dried cilantro

1 tablespoon lime juice

½ teaspoon salt

¼ cup sour cream (regular, low-fat, or nonfat)

¼ teaspoon ground cumin

1. Heat a medium saucepan over medium heat. Swirl in the oil, then stir in the onion and garlic. Cook for only 2 minutes, or just until the onion turns pale, stirring constantly. Raise the heat to medium-high and stir in the pork. Sauté for 2 more minutes, just until the meat is browned but not until it is cooked through.

2. Reserve ¾ cup of the garbanzo beans in a small bowl, then pour the remainder into the saucepan along with the chiles. Cook for 30 seconds, stirring constantly; then pour in the stock. Cover, reduce the heat to low, and cook for 40 minutes, stirring occasionally.

3. Remove 1 cup of the liquid from the saucepan. Place it along with the reserved garbanzo beans in a mini food processor, a regular food processor fitted with a chopping blade, or a large blender. Pulse until puréed, scraping down the sides of the bowl as necessary, then stir this puréed mixture into the soup. Continue simmering for 10 minutes, uncovered, stirring frequently.

4. Remove the pan from the heat and stir in the avocado, cilantro, lime juice, and salt. Cover and let rest off the heat for 5 minutes to meld the flavors. Meanwhile, whisk the sour cream and cumin in a small bowl until smooth.

5. To serve, stir the soup once, then divide it between two bowls. Top each with half the sour cream mixture.

PORK POSOLE 🍷🍷
makes 2 servings

A dish popular in Mexican and Tex-Mex cuisine, posole is a spicy but comforting stew of hominy and chiles, often served for dinner or breakfast alongside warm tortillas or a slab of fresh cornbread. No matter when it's made, it's usually long-simmered in an enormous pot, sometimes over an open fire. While a fire pit is not exactly practical when cooking for two, this stew can in fact be made relatively quickly on top of the stove using canned hominy. We've also substituted lean cuts of pork for the often-used pork shoulder, thereby reducing the cooking time further, and making the stew hearty without being fatty.

1 dried ancho chile (see page 8), cut in half, seeds and stem removed

2 tablespoons canola or other vegetable oil

1 small onion, minced

2 medium garlic cloves, minced

6 medium tomatillos (about 6 ounces total weight—see page 14), husks removed and discarded, flesh roughly chopped

¼ pound pork cutlet, pork loin, or pork tenderloin, trimmed and coarsely chopped

One 15½-ounce can hominy, drained and rinsed

One 14½-ounce can chicken stock (regular, low-fat, or nonfat, but preferably low-sodium)

1 tablespoon chopped fresh oregano, or 1 teaspoon dried oregano

1 teaspoon ground cumin

¼ teaspoon freshly ground black pepper

¼ cup fresh cilantro leaves, washed and roughly chopped, or 1 tablespoon dried cilantro

¼ teaspoon salt, or to taste

1. Heat a small, dry skillet or sauté pan over medium heat. Put in the ancho chile and toast for about 2 minutes, or until fiery fragrant, turning occasionally. Stand back—the oils in the chile may pop and sizzle. Transfer the toasted ancho to a cutting board, chop, and set aside.

2. Heat a medium saucepan over medium-high heat. Swirl in the oil, then toss in the onion, cooking it for about 2 minutes, or just until pale and softened, stirring frequently. Stir in the garlic, tomatillos, and pork; sauté for 2 more minutes, until the tomatillos begin to break down and the pork loses its raw pink color. Stir in the chopped ancho, the hominy, chicken stock, oregano, cumin, and pepper. Bring the mixture to a simmer; then cover, reduce the heat to low, and cook for 30 minutes, or until the pork is tender and the stew is slightly thickened, stirring occasionally.

3. Uncover the pan and cook for an additional 20 minutes to thicken the stew, stirring occasionally. Stir in the chopped cilantro, season with salt, and serve immediately.

The Sides
Top this hearty main-dish stew with any of the following:

> diced mango
> diced scallions
> diced tomatoes
> tortilla chips
> peeled and shredded jicama
> peeled and sliced avocados
> plain yogurt
> shredded Cheddar or Monterey Jack cheese
> sliced radishes
> sour cream (regular, low-fat, or nonfat)

YANKEE POT ROAST STEW

makes **2 hearty servings**

Or perhaps we should call this dish "pot roast in a bowl." It starts with a chuck roast, a soft buttery cut of beef that almost melts into the dish. As a balance of flavors, spiky-tasting turnips are added, as well as potatoes for earthiness. Dried cranberries give the dish a hint of sweetness. If you're not a fan of turnips, substitute a second 5-ounce potato and use 2 tablespoons unsalted butter, rather than the oil, to balance the flavors. All in all, this is a satisfying, one-pot meal for two.

2 tablespoons canola or other vegetable oil

¾ pound chuck roast, cut into 1-inch cubes

1 small onion, chopped

1 large garlic clove, minced

1 tablespoon all-purpose flour

One 14½-ounce can beef stock (regular, low-fat, or nonfat, but preferably low-sodium)

¼ cup dried cranberries, roughly chopped

1 bay leaf

½ teaspoon fresh thyme, or ¼ teaspoon dried thyme

¼ teaspoon freshly ground black pepper

1 medium turnip (about 6 ounces), peeled and cut into ½-inch cubes (about 1 cup)

1 medium yellow-fleshed potato (about 5 ounces), such as Yukon Gold, cut into ½-inch cubes (about 1 cup)

½ teaspoon salt

1. Heat a 3-quart pot over medium heat. Swirl in the oil, then drop in the cubed chuck roast. Cook for 3 minutes, just until browned, turning the cubes occasionally, then add the onion and garlic. Cook for 2 more minutes, or until the vegetables are pale and fragrant, stirring frequently.

2. Sprinkle the flour evenly over the meat and vegetables. Stir well, then cook for another 2 minutes, just until the flour begins to brown, stirring once or twice.

3. Stirring constantly, drizzle in the stock so that the flour dissolves and begins to thicken the stew. Once all the stock has been added, stir in the cranberries, bay leaf, thyme, and pepper. Cover, reduce the heat to very low, and simmer at the slowest bubble for 1 hour and 20 minutes, stirring occasionally.

4. Stir in the turnip and potato. Cover the pot again and simmer for an additional 20 minutes, or until the stew is thick and the meat is quite tender, stirring occasionally. Remove from the heat, cover, and let stand for 5 minutes to blend the flavors. Season with salt, then serve.

MOLE CHILI

makes **2 generous servings**

Mole is a dark, slightly bitter, somewhat sweet sauce made from chiles and aromatic herbs; it's now almost synonymous with the cooking from Oaxaca, Mexico. Mole may or may not include chocolate—culinary experts are still duking this one out—but our preference is distinctly for the chocolate variety. Here, we've simplified this classic sauce and turned it into a thick chili, perfect for a cold evening meal. The slight edge of unsweetened chocolate is the perfect foil to the ground meat and sweet beer in this winter warmer.

1 tablespoon canola or other vegetable oil
1 small onion, finely chopped
1 small green bell pepper, seeded, cored, and chopped
1 small garlic clove, minced
1/3 pound lean ground beef
1/3 pound ground pork
2 1/2 tablespoons chili powder (see page 8)
1 teaspoon ground cumin

2 teaspoons chopped fresh oregano, or 1 teaspoon dried oregano
One 12-ounce bottle beer, preferably a dark beer such as Negra Modelo or Bass
1/2 ounce unsweetened chocolate, chopped
1 tablespoon tomato paste (see page 14)
1/2 teaspoon salt, or to taste

1. Heat a medium saucepan over medium-high heat. Swirl in the oil, then stir in the onion and bell pepper and cook for about 3 minutes, or until soft and fragrant, stirring frequently. Add the garlic and cook for just 15 seconds; then crumble in the ground beef and pork. Cook for 2 minutes, just until the meat is lightly browned, stirring often.

2. Stir in the chili powder, cumin, and oregano; cook for 30 seconds to toast the spices, stirring constantly. (Do not stand over the pot—the volatilized chile oils may burn your eyes.) Stir in the beer and chocolate, and bring the mixture to a simmer. Cover, reduce the heat to low, and simmer for 15 minutes, stirring occasionally.

3. Stir in the tomato paste just until melted. Continue simmering for 15 minutes, partially covered, or until the chili is quite thick, stirring occasionally. Season with salt and serve immediately.

SUKIYAKI ⏱

makes **2 servings**

This version of the Japanese classic is so simple, you can add it to your weekly repertoire. Bring the sauté pan right to the table; then ladle the rich broth, vegetables, and meat into your bowls. Either type of noodle you choose is available in the Asian aisle of most supermarkets. Mung bean noodles are made from ground bean sprouts; yam starch noodles are made from a starchy white tuber grown in the mountains of northern Japan.

½ cup soy sauce (regular or low-sodium)
½ cup mirin (see Note)
¼ cup water
2 teaspoons sugar
1 tablespoon peanut oil
½ pound beef tenderloin, sliced into rounds as thin as possible
8 ounces firm tofu, cut into 1-inch cubes

6 ounces enoki mushrooms, bottoms trimmed, remaining mushrooms brushed clean and broken into 5 or 6 clumps
2 ounces dried mung bean noodles, or 2 ounces yam starch noodles (see headnote)
4 small scallions, cut into 3-inch pieces

1. Whisk the soy sauce, mirin, water, and sugar in a small saucepan set over medium-high heat until the sugar dissolves. Bring the mixture to a simmer, turn off the heat, and cover the pan to keep the mixture warm while you prepare the dish.

2. Heat a 10-inch high-sided sauté pan or cast-iron skillet over high heat until smoking. Swirl in the oil, then lay the tenderloin slices in the pan. Sear them for 10 seconds, turn, then sear for another 10 seconds. Reduce the heat to medium and mound the pieces of beef into one-quarter of the pan. Arrange the tofu, enoki, and noodles in the other quarters. Pour in the warmed soy sauce mixture, then mound the scallions in the center. Cover and bring the mixture to a simmer. Cook for 5 minutes, then serve.

NOTE: Mirin is a sweet cooking wine made from glutinous rice, sometimes sold under the name "sweetened rice wine." It's available in the Asian section of most supermarkets; read the label carefully and avoid brands loaded with MSG. If pressed, substitute sweet sherry.

Main Course Salads

Salads have long been on the short list of our small-batch repertoire. Unfortunately, they can also suffer from, well, a lack of imagination. So here is a set of salad recipes to break the boredom. Main courses all, they're perfect for summer evenings or weekend lunches, served up in portions for two. Look for medium tomatoes and small heads of lettuce that will allow you to make a fresh salad tonight without waste or leftovers. For the freshest taste, our best advice is to eat produce the day you buy it. That way, it stays out of the refrigerator, which indeed inhibits rot but also masks the flavors of fresh vegetables by causing their sugars and starches to break down. While a cool salad may be refreshing on a hot day, a room-temperature salad will always taste better.

SALADE AUX LARDONS SALAD
with POACHED EGG *and*
WARM BACON DRESSING 💼
makes 2 servings

In this classic bistro salad, torn pieces of frisée (also called curly endive—a feathery, peppery green) are topped with bacon and a poached egg. We've spiked the dressing with honey and mustard; otherwise, it's a quick, simple dinner, ready in minutes. Look for tight, compact frisée heads, with green tips and a pure white base to the leaves. The ratio of green to white indicates the relative bitterness of the frisée: less white means less astringent frisée. Slab bacon is often available shrink-wrapped in the meat section or directly from your butcher.

½ pound slab bacon, cut into
½-inch pieces
1 medium shallot, thinly sliced
1½ tablespoons plus
¼ teaspoon white wine
vinegar
1 teaspoon Dijon mustard
1 teaspoon honey

½ teaspoon freshly ground
black pepper
2 large eggs, at room
temperature
1 small head frisée or curly
endive (about 9 ounces),
torn into bite-sized pieces
(about 3 packed cups)

1. Spread the bacon pieces evenly in a medium skillet, then place the skillet over low heat. When the bacon begins to sizzle, stir it well, then sauté for about 15 minutes, or until crispy and irresistible. Don't be tempted to raise the heat: the low cooking temperature will help render the fat. Using a slotted spoon, transfer the bacon from the skillet to a plate lined with paper towels, but keep the fat in the pan.

2. Raise the heat to medium, add the shallot, and cook for 2 minutes, or until fragrant. Remove the skillet from the heat and whisk the 1½ tablespoons vinegar, the mustard, honey, and pepper right into the pan, mixing until the dressing is thick, slightly opaque, and emulsified. Set aside on the stove to keep warm.

3. Bring a medium saucepan filled halfway with water to a boil over high heat. Crack each of the eggs into two small bowls or teacups. Stir the remaining ¼ teaspoon of vinegar into the boiling water, then slip the eggs from the bowls into the pan. Cover and poach the eggs for about 3 minutes, or just until the yolks are set. Meanwhile, divide the frisée between two dinner plates. Top with the crispy bacon.

4. Using a slotted spoon, transfer one poached egg to each of the two plates, placing the eggs on top of the salad. Rewhisk the dressing, then drizzle half over each salad. Serve immediately.

PORK SATAY SALAD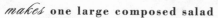

makes one large composed salad

Satay is an everyday street food of Southeast Asia. Technically, it's marinated strips of meat, skewered and grilled over an open fire. The marinade is sweet, a little sour, peppery with ginger and chiles, and quite irresistible. We've turned that classic marinade into a dressing for this light, refreshing salad, topped with marinated pork tenderloin and sprinkled with mint, peanuts, and coconut.

⅓ cup lime juice (juice of 3 to 4 medium limes; see Note)

2 tablespoons peeled, minced fresh ginger

1½ tablespoons packed light brown sugar

1½ tablespoons nam pla (see page 10)

1 tablespoon peanut oil

1 teaspoon red chili paste (see page 12)

1 small garlic clove, minced

1 small pork tenderloin (about ½ pound), trimmed and sliced into ½-inch rounds

1 small head Bibb lettuce (about 10 ounces), washed and torn (about 4 cups)

½ cup thinly sliced radishes (about 4 large radishes)

¼ cup fresh cilantro leaves, washed (do not use dried herbs)

3 tablespoons chopped fresh mint leaves

2 tablespoons chopped roasted unsalted peanuts

1½ tablespoons unsweetened shredded coconut

1. To make the satay marinade, whisk the lime juice, ginger, brown sugar, nam pla, peanut oil, red chili paste, and garlic in a medium bowl until the sugar dissolves.

2. Place the pork tenderloin slices in a separate medium bowl. Spoon 6 tablespoons of the marinade over the sliced pork, toss well to coat, then cover and set aside at room temperature for 20 minutes, stirring occasionally. Reserve the remaining lime juice marinade as a dressing for the salad.

3. Place the broiling rack or a lipped baking sheet 4 to 6 inches from the heat source; preheat the broiler. You can line the rack or the baking sheet with aluminum foil to facilitate cleanup later on. Without draining them, lay the marinated pork slices on the rack and broil for 5 minutes, until browned and cooked through, turning once. Discard the marinade they've been soaking in.

4. Gently toss the lettuce, radishes, cilantro, and mint on a serving platter until well combined. Sprinkle with the peanuts and coconut; top with the cooked pork slices. Spoon the reserved lime juice mixture over the platter as the dressing. Serve immediately.

> N O T E : To get the most juice out of citrus fruits, make sure they're at room temperature. Before cutting them open, roll them along your work surface, firmly pressing down with the palm of your hand.

SOUTHWESTERN SALAD *with* CHICKEN, GRAPEFRUIT, *and* CUMIN VINAIGRETTE 🍷🍷

makes one large composed salad

The flavors of this salad were inspired by the best of Texas cooking—pecans, whole cumin seeds, chiles, and ruby red grapefruits, a Rio Grande Valley specialty. The various ingredients are prepared separately, then assembled at the last minute on a serving platter; a zesty dressing, made with heart-healthy grapeseed oil, is drizzled over the top. Serve this salad with flour or corn tortillas warmed in the microwave for a minute on high.

FOR THE DRESSING

1 teaspoon whole cumin seeds
¼ teaspoon red pepper flakes
2 tablespoons red wine vinegar
1 garlic clove, crushed
¼ teaspoon salt, or to taste
5 tablespoons grapeseed oil, or olive oil

FOR THE SALAD

1 small red bell pepper
2 teaspoons lime juice
1 tablespoon chili powder (see page 8)
2 boneless, skinless chicken breast halves (about ¾ pound total weight)

1 tablespoon grapeseed oil, or olive oil
1 ear corn, kernels removed, cob discarded
¼ cup pecan pieces
1 medium ruby red grapefruit
1 small head Boston lettuce, stemmed, washed, dried, leaves torn into bite-sized chunks
1 small shallot, thinly sliced and broken into rings (see Notes, page 54)
2 tablespoons chopped fresh cilantro (do not use dried)

1. To make the dressing, toast the cumin seeds and the red pepper flakes in a small dry skillet set over medium heat for 2 minutes, or until very fragrant. Stand back: the chile oils can volatilize and burn your eyes. Set the spices aside in the skillet while you whisk the vinegar, garlic, and salt in a small bowl. Whisk in the oil in a thin, steady stream;

continue whisking until the dressing thickens. Transfer the spices to a cutting board; lightly crush them with the side of a large knife. Stir the spices into the dressing, then set aside.

2. Char the bell pepper by holding it with long-handled tongs over an open gas flame, or place it on the broiler rack or a baking sheet 4 to 6 inches from a preheated broiler. Turn the pepper until charred on all sides, including the top and bottom. Drop it into a paper bag and seal the bag; or place it in a small bowl and cover the bowl tightly with plastic wrap. Set aside to steam for about 20 minutes.

3. Meanwhile, use a small whisk or a fork to mix the lime juice and chili powder in a small bowl until they form a paste. Massage this paste onto the chicken breasts. Heat a medium skillet over medium-high heat. Swirl in the oil, then lay the chicken breasts in the skillet. Cook for about 5 minutes, or until browned; then turn and cook for about 5 more minutes, or until cooked through and deeply browned. Transfer to a plate, tent with foil to keep warm, and set aside.

4. Rinse and dry the skillet, then set it over medium heat. Add the corn and pecans; sauté for about 3 minutes, or until the nuts are fragrant and the corn is lightly browned. Set aside.

5. To cut the grapefruit into supremes, cut off its bottom (so it can stand steady on the counter), then use a paring knife to cut the rind off the flesh in long arcs, starting at the top and following the natural curve of the fruit. Cut down far enough to remove the white pith, but not so far as to damage the fruit membranes. Once peeled, hold the grapefruit in your hand and use the paring knife to cut between the pink flesh and the white pith separating the individual segments. Allow the segments to fall into a bowl. Set them aside; discard any pith and peel.

6. Remove the charred pepper from the bag or bowl; peel off the blackened skin with your fingers. Do not run water over the pepper—water will make it soggy. Core and seed the pepper, then slice it into thin strips. The salad can be made up to this point up to 6 hours ahead of time. Cover the various ingredients separately; store the cooled chicken in the refrigerator, but let it come back to room temperature before proceeding.

7. On a serving platter, toss the lettuce, shallot, and cilantro. Top with the pepper strips, grapefruit supremes, toasted corn, and peanuts. Slice the chicken breast into ½-inch strips and lay them on top of the greens. Whisk the prepared dressing to reincorporate any oil that has fallen out of suspension; drizzle this dressing over the salad. Serve immediately.

CUMIN MAYONNAISE DRESSING

If you prefer a mayonnaise dressing, toast the cumin seeds and red pepper flakes as directed, but omit the remainder of the ingredients for the dressing. Mix the crushed, toasted seeds and red pepper flakes in a small bowl along with ½ cup mayonnaise (regular, low-fat, or nonfat), ¼ cup purchased salsa, and 1 teaspoon lime juice. Dot this dressing over the salad on the serving platter. This mayonnaise dressing can be made up to 2 days in advance; store it, covered, in the refrigerator, but allow it to come back to room temperature before serving.

Soba Noodle Chicken Salad

makes **2 servings**

Cooked soba noodles, a Japanese favorite made from buckwheat flour, are a little chewier than Italian pasta, so they're perfect for cold salads, a good contrast to the crisp, crunchy vegetables. The dressing for this salad is a fusion of flavors: soy sauce and ginger, thickened with tahini, and spiced up with Tabasco sauce. Soba noodles are usually available dried in supermarkets and gourmet stores; if you find fresh noodles, buy 6 ounces and cook them only for a few seconds in a pot of boiling water.

FOR THE SALAD

2 small boneless, skinless chicken breast halves (about 4 ounces each)

2 teaspoons olive oil

½ teaspoon salt

¼ teaspoon freshly ground black pepper

1 small shallot, sliced paper thin, then broken into rings (see Notes)

1 small red bell pepper, cored, seeded, and cut into thin strips

1 small cucumber, peeled, seeded, and diced

3 tablespoons chopped peanuts

2 tablespoons chopped fresh cilantro, or 1 tablespoon dried cilantro

4 ounces dried soba noodles (see headnote), cooked and drained according to package instructions

FOR THE DRESSING

2 tablespoons tahini (see Notes)

2 tablespoons soy sauce

2 tablespoons rice vinegar (see page 12)

2 teaspoons peeled, minced fresh ginger

1 teaspoon sesame oil

1 small garlic clove, minced

2 dashes Tabasco sauce, or more to taste

1. To prepare the chicken, position the broiler rack or a baking sheet 4 to 6 inches from the heat source and preheat the broiler. You can cover the rack or baking sheet with aluminum foil to speed cleanup. Massage the oil into the breasts, then season them with salt and pepper. Lay them on the heated rack or baking sheet and broil for 6 minutes, or until browned. Turn, then broil for about 6 more minutes, or until cooked through but still moist. Alternatively, grill them over medium-high heat or medium-high-heat coals for 12 minutes, turning once.

2. Cool the chicken breasts at room temperature for 5 minutes, then slice them into thin strips. Place the strips in a large serving bowl. Toss with the shallot, bell pepper, cucumber, peanuts, and cilantro. Add the noodles and toss.

3. To make the dressing, whisk the tahini, soy sauce, rice vinegar, ginger, garlic, sesame oil, and Tabasco sauce in a medium bowl until uniform. Pour the dressing over the salad, toss gently, then serve immediately.

> **NOTES:** You can use a mandoline to slice a shallot paper thin. Hold the shallot with the gripping device and run it smoothly across the cutting blade, adjusted to a paper-thin setting.
>
> Tahini is a paste made from untoasted sesame seeds. It's available in many supermarkets and most health food stores. It's best to buy it in clear jars, rather than cans, so you can see how fresh it is. It should look rusty beige, not a blackened brown, and be smooth, not grainy. To preserve its freshness, store tahini, covered, in the refrigerator for up to a year. If the oil separates from the paste, stir with a wooden spoon to reincorporate.

CURRIED TUNA STUFFED TOMATOES

makes **2 stuffed tomatoes**

These are not your mother's stuffed tomatoes. But her bridge club would certainly be envious of this light lunch or dinner, the tuna seasoned with curry powder for kick and studded with cashews, cranberries, and fresh ginger. Stuffed tomatoes are the perfect meal when you'd rather not turn on the oven.

2 tablespoons roughly chopped unsalted cashews

One 6-ounce can water-packed tuna, drained (and rinsed, if desired)

1 small celery rib, minced

1 small scallion, white part only, minced

3 tablespoons mayonnaise (regular, low-fat, or nonfat)

2 tablespoons dried cranberries or dried cherries

1½ teaspoons curry powder

½ teaspoon peeled, minced fresh ginger

¼ teaspoon salt

2 large tomatoes (about 12 ounces each)

1. Toast the chopped cashews in a small, dry skillet set over low heat for about 3 minutes, until lightly browned, stirring frequently. Cool, then place them in a medium bowl. Stir in the tuna, celery, scallion, mayonnaise, cranberries, curry powder, ginger, and salt. Set aside.

2. Cut a small slice from the bottom of each tomato so it will stand up on a plate. Turn them over and core each by making a ½-inch-deep well around the remnants of the stem with a paring knife; continue enlarging that hole with the paring knife until the tomato is cored. Use a spoon to scoop out some of the flesh, removing flesh and seeds about halfway down the inside, but leaving a ¼-inch wall around the sides.

3. Stuff each with half of the curried tuna mixture. Serve immediately; or store, covered, in the refrigerator for up to 24 hours.

SEAFOOD SALAD 💼

makes **2 servings**

Don't let the number of ingredients put you off: this salad is as trouble-free as it is elegant. The shrimp and scallops cook in no time, the lump crabmeat is ready-to-eat when purchased, and the rest of the preparation involves cutting up the vegetables and whisking up an easy dressing. In the end, you'll have a fresh, light shellfish salad with orange sections and avocado slices, all dressed with a peppery vinaigrette.

1 small shallot, minced

2 tablespoons Champagne vinegar or white wine vinegar

1 tablespoon lime juice (the juice of about 1 small lime)

1 teaspoon Dijon mustard

½ teaspoon salt, or to taste

½ teaspoon freshly ground black pepper

¼ cup plus 1 tablespoon olive oil

2 dashes Tabasco sauce, or to taste

4 ounces small shrimp (about 12 shrimp at 45 per pound), peeled and deveined, then cut in half lengthwise

3 ounces sea scallops (about 3 large scallops), sliced into ¼-inch disks

6 ounces lump crabmeat, picked over for shells and cartilage (see Notes)

1 medium orange

1 small Hass avocado (see Notes)

1 small head Romaine lettuce (about 8 ounces), cored and shredded (about 3 packed cups)

1. To make the dressing, mix the shallot, vinegar, lime juice, mustard, salt, and pepper in a small bowl. Drizzle in the olive oil, whisking all the while; continue whisking until creamy and smooth. Stir in the Tabasco sauce, then set aside.

2. Prepare a small bowl of ice water and set it aside. Bring a small saucepan of salted water to boil over high heat. Add the shrimp and scallops to the simmering water and poach for about 2 minutes, just until the shrimp are firm and pink. Drain, then place the shellfish in the ice water. Let stand for 2 minutes, then drain and place the cooked shellfish in a serving bowl. Stir in the crabmeat.

3. Cut ¼ inch off the top and bottom of the orange, so that it will sit flat. Stand it on a cutting board, then cut down the sides of the fruit with a paring knife, following the fruit's natural curve, removing the rind and the white pith underneath. (You may also cut off a small amount of the flesh.) Hold the fruit in one hand over a small bowl. Use a paring knife to cut between the membranes, letting the orange supremes and any juice fall into the bowl. Take care not to squeeze the orange, thereby juicing it and rendering the supremes dry. Discard any remaining pith and add the supremes and any juice to the serving bowl with the seafood.

4. Cut the avocado in half, remove the pit, then peel each half. A large serving spoon can easily scoop half an avocado out of its peel. Cut the avocado into ½-inch pieces; add them to the seafood salad.

5. Whisk the dressing once again to incorporate any oil that has fallen out of suspension. Pour the dressing over the seafood salad. Add the shredded lettuce and toss gently using tongs or two large spoons. Serve immediately.

> **NOTES:** Cooked lump crabmeat is often available fresh in your fishmonger's refrigerated case. It also comes in cans, but the taste can be quite fishy. The fresh variety is preferable for this salad—but check the expiration date and buy the freshest you can find.
>
> To pick the crabmeat over for shells and cartilage, spread it out on a plate without breaking it up too much—you'll be able to see any fragments still in the meat. You can also run your fingers lightly across the meat, but be careful: you can get pierced.
>
> Choose an avocado that is dark-skinned but still firm—that is, slightly underripe. Too ripe, and the avocado will become mushy in the salad.

TABBOULEH *with* SHRIMP, FETA, *and* DILL

makes 2 servings

Traditionally, tabbouleh is a Middle Eastern salad made with bulgur wheat, mint, and fresh tomatoes. Here's a version shifted a little to Greece, with feta, dill, shrimp, and sundried tomatoes.

½ cup bulgur wheat
½ cup boiling water
⅓ pound medium shrimp
  (about 10 shrimp at 30 per
  pound), peeled and
  deveined
½ cup crumbled feta
  (about 2 ounces)
¼ cup chopped sundried
  tomatoes (see Note)
1 small scallion, thinly sliced

¼ cup chopped fresh dill, or
  2 tablespoons dried dill
¼ cup packed chopped fresh
  parsley, or 1½ tablespoons
  dried parsley
2 tablespoons olive oil
2 tablespoons lemon juice
½ teaspoon salt
½ teaspoon freshly ground
  black pepper

1. Place the bulgur in a small bowl; stir in the boiling water. Set aside for 30 minutes, or until the water is absorbed and the bulgur is tender.

2. Meanwhile, bring a small saucepan of salted water to a boil over high heat. Add the shrimp and cook for about 2 minutes, just until pink and firm. Drain and cool the shrimp, then roughly chop them and place them in a medium serving bowl.

3. Fluff the bulgur with a fork, then add it to the shrimp. Stir in the feta, sundried tomatoes, scallion, dill, parsley, olive oil, lemon juice, salt, and pepper. Toss gently, then serve.

NOTE: The sundried tomatoes should be soft and pliable. If yours are leathery and hard, rehydrate them in a small bowl of hot water for 3 minutes. You can also buy sundried tomatoes packed in oil, but drain, rinse, and blot them dry before using them in this salad.

QUINOA SALAD with RED ONION, CUCUMBER, and WALNUTS ⏱

makes 2 servings

This savory salad is made with quinoa (KEEN-wah), an ancient grain from South America. A grain of quinoa is tiny—when cooked, it looks like a beige poppy seed with a small, translucent halo. The cooking technique for quinoa is similar to rice, although it's simmered for a shorter time. If you don't want to buy a box of quinoa at your market, it's often sold in bulk at health food stores.

⅓ cup walnut pieces

2 cups water

⅔ cup quinoa

1 small cucumber, peeled, halved lengthwise, seeds scraped out, remainder chopped

1 small red onion, minced

2 tablespoons peeled, minced fresh ginger

2 tablespoons Champagne vinegar or white wine vinegar

2 tablespoons olive oil, preferably extra-virgin olive oil

2 tablespoons chopped fresh parsley, or 2 teaspoons dried parsley

1 teaspoon sesame oil

½ teaspoon salt, or to taste

¼ teaspoon freshly ground black pepper

1. Toast the walnuts in a small, dry skillet set over medium heat for about 3 minutes, or until lightly browned and quite fragrant. Transfer them to a cutting board and roughly chop them. Place in a medium serving bowl.

2. Bring the water to a boil in a small saucepan set over high heat. Stir in the quinoa, cover the pan, reduce the heat to low, and simmer for 10 minutes, until tender. Set aside to steep off the heat for 5 minutes, then transfer the cooked quinoa to a serving bowl. (All the water should have been incorporated. If not—because of the quinoa's density or the day's humidity—drain the quinoa before adding it to the bowl.)

3. Stir in the cucumber, onion, ginger, vinegar, olive oil, parsley, sesame oil, salt, and pepper. Serve immediately; or store, covered, in the refrigerator for up to 3 days. If stored, stir thoroughly and allow to come back to room temperature before serving.

Casseroles

Casseroles, it seems, are designed to make us think in grand numbers: 9 × 13, 11 × 17. We picture a huge baking dish, family-sized portions, hot, bubbling, and very homey. So why do we need to throw out these childhood pleasures with the baking dish? Casseroles need hardly be the imperial things they've become. They're simply one-baking-dish meals, sometimes baked in the oven, sometimes on the stovetop, the filling either set (with cheese or eggs, for example) or somehow thickened. In this chapter, we start with the family classics, some of them admittedly retro, such as Macaroni and Cheese or Turkey Tetrazzini; then we move on to the classics, such as Arroz con Pollo and Stuffed Baked Potatoes, perhaps the best casserole of all, the potato skins serving as the baking dish to hold a rich, creamy filling. So save the 11 × 17-inch baking dish for another day and make a warm, satisfying casserole tonight—but this time, without the waste or the leftovers.

MACARONI *and* CHEESE 🧳
makes a 1-quart casserole

What could be more comforting than mac and cheese? Problem is, it loses some of its appeal by the third day. So here's a version of that family favorite for two—made with Cheddar, of course, for that classic velvety richness, but also with Parmigiano-Reggiano, for a little tangy finish with every bite. A simple tossed salad would be the best accompaniment for this all-American meal.

3 tablespoons unsalted butter, plus additional for buttering the baking dish

1 small onion, finely chopped

2 tablespoons all-purpose flour

2 cups milk (regular, low-fat, or nonfat)

⅔ cup shredded Cheddar (about 5 ounces)

1 teaspoon dry mustard

¼ teaspoon freshly ground black pepper

⅛ teaspoon salt

2 dashes Tabasco sauce, or to taste

6 ounces dry elbow macaroni, cooked according to package instructions

¼ cup grated Parmigiano-Reggiano (about 1 ounce)

1. Position the rack in the center of the oven and preheat the oven to 350°F. Butter a 1-quart round soufflé dish or a 1-quart shallow casserole. (A soufflé dish will produce a creamier casserole; a shallow dish, a crunchier one).

2. Melt 3 tablespoons of the butter in a medium saucepan set over medium heat. Reduce the heat to very low, stir in the onion, and cook for 5 minutes, until soft and golden, stirring frequently. Don't let the onion brown, if at all possible—this will keep the final dish creamy white. Whisk in the flour and cook for 15 seconds, just so that the flour loses its raw taste. Do not brown the flour. Whisk in the milk in a steady, slow stream. Raise the heat to medium and continue cooking and whisking for about 1 minute, or until the mixture returns to a boil and thickens.

3. Reduce the heat to low and stir in the Cheddar, dry mustard, pepper, salt, and Tabasco sauce. Continue cooking for 2 more minutes, or until the cheese melts and the mixture is smooth, stirring constantly. Finally, stir in the cooked macaroni and grated Parmigiano-Reggiano, then pour this mixture into the prepared casserole dish.

4. Bake for 30 minutes, or until bubbly and lightly browned. If desired, place the casserole under a preheated broiler for about 20 seconds to further brown the top. Let stand for 5 minutes, then serve.

Cheese Shop Mac and Cheese

Substitute any number of cheeses to update this classic. For the Cheddar, substitute equivalent amounts of chopped Brie, grated Gruyère, or chopped Havarti. For the Parmigiano-Reggiano, substitute equivalent amounts of Gorgonzola, Camembert, or Asiago. You can also add spices along with the dry mustard to the sauce. Try one of the following: ½ teaspoon dried dill, ¼ teaspoon grated nutmeg, or ¼ teaspoon ground allspice.

A Bread-Crumb Topping

Some people like the crunchiness of the macaroni as it browns in the oven. Others prefer to add their own crunch with a topping. To do so, simply mix ⅓ cup plain dried bread crumbs, 1 tablespoon unsalted butter, melted, 1 teaspoon dried parsley, and ¼ teaspoon salt in a small bowl, then sprinkle this mixture over the mac and cheese after it has baked for 10 minutes. Continue baking about 25 more minutes, or until the bread crumb topping is deeply browned and the cheesy filling is bubbling through the crust.

TUNA NOODLE CASSEROLE

makes a 1-quart casserole

Cut down to size and updated with artichoke hearts, this family favorite is still right any night of the week.

2 tablespoons plus 1 teaspoon unsalted butter, plus additional for buttering the casserole dish

1 small shallot, minced

1 tablespoon all-purpose flour

1 cup milk (regular, low-fat, or nonfat)

2 tablespoons chopped fresh parsley, or 2 teaspoons dried parsley

1 teaspoon Dijon mustard

¼ teaspoon salt

¼ teaspoon freshly ground black pepper

One 7-ounce jar water-packed artichoke hearts, drained, rinsed, and chopped

One 6-ounce can water-packed chunk white tuna, drained (and rinsed, if desired)

3 ounces dried egg noodles, cooked according to package instructions

2 tablespoons grated Cheddar (about ½ ounce)

1 tablespoon plain dried bread crumbs

1. Position the rack in the center of the oven and preheat the oven to 400°F. Butter a 1-quart round soufflé dish.

2. Melt 2 tablespoons of the butter in a large skillet or sauté pan set over medium heat. Add the shallot and cook for 2 minutes, just until soft and golden, stirring frequently. Sprinkle the flour evenly over the shallot and cook for about 15 seconds, just so that the flour loses its raw taste, but not so long that it begins to brown. Whisk in the milk in a slow, steady stream. Continue whisking over medium heat until the mixture thickens and boils, about 1 minute; then whisk in the parsley, mustard, salt, and pepper.

3. Remove the skillet from the heat; stir in the artichoke hearts, tuna, and cooked noodles. Pour this mixture into the prepared casserole dish. Sprinkle the cheese over the top, dust on the bread crumbs, and dot with the remaining 1 teaspoon butter.

4. Bake for 20 minutes, or until bubbly and lightly browned. If desired, place the casserole under a preheated broiler for about 20 seconds to further brown the top. Let stand at room temperature for 5 minutes before serving.

BEEF and MAC CASSEROLE ⏱

makes a 1-quart casserole

Food snobs, look elsewhere. Long a lunchroom favorite and the inspiration for countless packaged imitators, beef and mac casserole has passed into the realm of American culinary icons. Why not try it again? While it bakes, pour yourself a glass of iced tea and watch the evening news. Soon enough, you'll have a warm, comforting meal, best served with corn muffins. For dessert? Ice cream sundaes, of course.

1 tablespoon olive oil
1 small onion, minced
1 medium celery rib, chopped
1 medium garlic clove, minced
½ pound lean ground beef, preferably ground sirloin
One 15-ounce can tomato sauce
2 teaspoons chopped fresh oregano, or 1 teaspoon dried oregano
2 teaspoons chopped fresh basil, or 1 teaspoon dried basil

¼ teaspoon salt
¼ teaspoon freshly ground black pepper
3 ounces dried elbow macaroni, cooked according to package instructions
¼ cup grated Cheddar, or ¼ cup freshly grated Parmigiano-Reggiano (about 1 ounce)

1. Position the rack in the middle of the oven and preheat the oven to 350°F.

2. Heat a large skillet or sauté pan over medium-high heat. Swirl in the oil, then stir in the onion and celery and cook for 2 minutes, or until somewhat limp but fragrant, stirring frequently. Stir in the garlic and cook for only 10 seconds, just until it sizzles at the edges. Then crumble the beef into the pan and cook for about 5 minutes, or until lightly browned, stirring occasionally.

3. Pour in the tomato sauce, stir well, and add the oregano, basil, salt, and pepper. Bring the mixture to a simmer. Cover, reduce the heat to medium-low, and cook for 5 minutes. Stir in the cooked macaroni and 2 tablespoons of the grated cheese. Pour this mixture into a 1-quart round soufflé dish. Top with the remaining 2 tablespoons of cheese.

4. Bake for 30 minutes, or until bubbly and lightly browned. Let stand for 5 minutes at room temperature before serving.

Making a Classic More Interesting

Stir 2 tablespoons powdered dried mushrooms, such as porcini or chanterelles, into the beef mixture with the macaroni.

Or omit the Cheddar and stir 2 tablespoons Gorgonzola, Asiago, Havarti, or feta into the beef mixture with the macaroni. Top the dish with 2 tablespoons of freshly grated Parmigiano-Reggiano.

COWBOY BAKED BEANS

makes 2 servings

A dish of baked beans is hardly a meal in itself—although we've often wished it could be! It's a childhood favorite, really—those tender beans simmering in that sweet, salty sauce. It ought to be an adult favorite, too—so here it is, updated with fresh tomatoes, beer, and beef jerky, which lends the dish a salty, piquant bite. Call it a campfire treat brought indoors.

1 tablespoon canola or other vegetable oil
½ pound lean ground beef
1 small onion, minced
1 medium garlic clove, minced
1 teaspoon all-purpose flour
1 ounce beef jerky, chopped
1 Italian plum tomato, chopped
2 tablespoons ketchup
2 tablespoons packed dark brown sugar
1½ teaspoons dry mustard
1½ teaspoons cider vinegar

½ teaspoon freshly ground black pepper
¼ teaspoon salt
One 15-ounce can pinto beans, rinsed and drained
One 12-ounce bottle beer, preferably a dark beer (but not a flavored beer)
¼ teaspoon liquid smoke, optional
3 dashes Tabasco sauce, or to taste

1. Position the rack in the center of the oven and preheat the oven to 400°F.

2. Heat a medium oven-safe pot or Dutch oven over medium-high heat. Swirl in the oil, then crumble in the ground beef. Sauté for only about 1 minute, just until it loses its raw, red color; then add the onion and cook for 1 minute, stirring constantly to incorporate the onion into the meat. Add the garlic and cook for just 10 seconds, stirring constantly.

3. Sprinkle the flour evenly over the beef mixture, and cook for 30 seconds undisturbed. Stir well, then cook for 1 more minute, stirring the mixture once or twice while browning the flour slightly. Stir in the beef jerky and tomato; cook for about 2 minutes, or just until the mixture comes to a simmer and the tomatoes start to break down. Once they do, stir in the ketchup, brown sugar, dry mustard, vinegar, pepper, and salt. Cook for about 10 seconds, or until the spices become aromatic; then stir in the beans, beer, liquid smoke (if using), and Tabasco sauce. Bring the mixture back to a simmer and cook for 3 minutes, stirring constantly.

4. Place the pot in the oven and bake, uncovered, for about 55 minutes, or until thick and bubbly, stirring occasionally to prevent sticking. Let stand for 5 minutes at room temperature before serving.

Warming Tortillas
This casserole is best with flour or corn tortillas. To heat them, wrap them in foil and place them in the preheated 400°F oven for 5 minutes, while the casserole stands at room temperature.

TAMALE PIE 💼

No list of casserole favorites would be complete without tamale pie: a rich, spicy pork ragoût, baked under a cornmeal crust. Our version uses a lean cut of pork (to cut down on the fat) and sliced zucchini (to add moisture back to the baked dish, moisture usually supplied by fattier cuts of pork). Make the filling before you make the crust—the cornmeal will harden even at room temperature if allowed to stand unattended. Nonetheless, make sure the crust is starting to firm up even before you spoon it onto the dish. If it doesn't—because of the day's humidity, most likely—add a little extra cornmeal to the mixture for firmness.

3 tablespoons canola or other
    vegetable oil
1 small onion, chopped
1 green Anaheim pepper,
    cored, seeded, and chopped
    (see Note)
1 small garlic clove, minced
1/2 pound pork cutlets, or
    1/2 pound boneless pork
    chops, or 1/2 pound pork
    loin, any of these cut into
    1/2-inch cubes
1 small zucchini, halved
    lengthwise, and cut into
    1/2-inch-thick half-moons

1 1/2 teaspoons chili powder
1/2 teaspoon ground cumin
1/2 teaspoon salt
1/4 teaspoon ground cinnamon
One 14 1/2-ounce can diced
    tomatoes
2 tablespoons chopped fresh
    cilantro, or 2 teaspoons
    dried cilantro
1 1/2 cups water
1/2 cup yellow cornmeal

1. Position the rack in the bottom third of the oven and preheat the oven to 350°F.

2. Heat a large skillet or sauté pan over medium-high heat. Swirl in 1 tablespoon of the oil, then toss in the onion and cook for 3 minutes, or until soft and aromatic, stirring frequently. Stir in the chopped pepper and garlic; cook for 30 seconds, stirring constantly. Stir in the diced pork and cook for about 2 more minutes, or just until the meat loses its pink color, stirring occasionally.

3. Stir in the diced zucchini and cook for 1 minute, just until slightly limp. Stir in the chili powder, cumin, ¼ teaspoon of the salt, and the cinnamon; continue cooking for about 20 seconds. Once the spices are fragrant, stir in the tomatoes (and their juice) and the cilantro, then bring the mixture to a boil undisturbed. Cover, reduce the heat to low, and simmer for 5 minutes, stirring once or twice. Pour this mixture into a shallow 1-quart casserole dish; set aside.

4. Bring the water, the remaining 2 tablespoons of oil, and the remaining ¼ teaspoon of salt to a full boil in a small saucepan set over high heat. Reduce the heat to medium, and sprinkle the cornmeal into the still-boiling water in a slow, steady, thin stream, just a few grains at a time, stirring constantly. Once all the cornmeal has been added, reduce the heat to low and continue cooking for about 3 minutes, or until thick but very smooth, stirring constantly. If the mixture dried out too quickly or is sandy in texture, add additional water in 1 tablespoon increments until smooth, like cooked Cream of Wheat. Remove the pan from the heat and let the cornmeal stand for about 1 minute, just until you can tell it's starting to firm up. Spoon the mixture over the pork filling in the casserole dish, gently spreading it over the dish to create a top crust.

5. Place the casserole on a lipped baking sheet to catch any drips. Bake for 30 minutes, or until the crust is lightly browned and the filling is bubbling up around the edges. Let stand for 5 minutes at room temperature before serving.

NOTE: Anaheim peppers are 6 to 8 inches long, quite narrow, and light green. When matured, they turn deep red and are called New Mexican red chiles. Substitute a milder cubanel (Italian frying pepper) or even a small green bell pepper, seeded, cored, and chopped, if you desire.

The Sides

Once the casserole's dished up into bowls, you can top it with one or several of the following, if you wish:

diced avocado
diced tomatoes
garlic or radish sprouts
pickled jalapeño pepper slices
purchased salsa
shredded Cheddar
shredded jicama
shredded lettuce
sliced radishes
sour cream

TURKEY TETRAZZINI ⏱

makes a 1-quart casserole

This long-time lunchroom favorite still has a place in our smaller baking dishes. Better yet, we've updated it a bit with a thickened mushroom broth rather than a palate-drenching cream sauce. While some versions make the dish on top of the stove, we've stuck with the original '50s method of baking the casserole in the oven, where the flavors have a chance to meld and deepen. That way, you won't even notice the missing cream.

½ ounce dried shiitake mushrooms (about 9 mushrooms—do not use fresh; see page 9)

¾ cup boiling water

1½ tablespoons unsalted butter

½ pound turkey breast fillet or turkey scaloppini, sliced into ½-inch strips

2 teaspoons all-purpose flour

¼ cup nonfat sour cream (see Note)

1 tablespoon dry sherry or dry vermouth

1 teaspoon Dijon mustard

¼ teaspoon salt

¼ teaspoon freshly ground pepper, preferably white pepper

2 medium scallions, thinly sliced

¼ cup grated Cheddar, or ¼ cup freshly grated Parmigiano-Reggiano (about 1 ounce)

4 ounces dried spaghetti, cooked according to the package instructions

1. Place the dried shiitakes in a medium bowl and cover them with the boiling water. Set aside to soak for about 15 minutes, or until soft. Position the rack in the center of the oven and preheat the oven to 350°F.

2. Drain the mushrooms, reserving the liquid. (The liquid may be sandy. If so, strain it through a colander lined with cheesecloth or paper towels.) Rinse the mushrooms, removing any sand from their gills by running your fingers across them under running water. Cut off their stems and discard; thinly slice the caps.

3. Melt ½ tablespoon of the butter in a medium skillet or sauté pan over medium heat. Add the turkey strips and sauté for about 2 minutes, or just until no longer pink. Transfer the strips to a plate and return the skillet to medium heat.

4. Melt the remaining 1 tablespoon of butter in the skillet. Sprinkle the flour evenly over the melted butter, let the flour stand in the sizzling butter for 10 seconds, then whisk to combine. Once it's pastelike, begin whisking in the reserved, strained mushroom soaking liquid in a slow, steady stream. Continue whisking and cooking for about 20 seconds, or just until the mixture returns to a boil and begins to thicken.

5. Whisk in the sour cream, sherry, mustard, salt, pepper, and scallions. Cook for only 10 seconds, just until heated through; then stir in the sliced mushrooms, the turkey strips, any juice accumulated on the plate, and 2 tablespoons of the grated cheese. Remove the pan from the heat and stir in the cooked spaghetti. Pour this mixture into a 1-quart round soufflé dish and top with the remaining 2 tablespoons of cheese.

6. Bake for 25 minutes, or until the casserole is bubbly and the cheese is melted. Let stand at room temperature for 5 minutes before serving.

NOTE: Use only nonfat sour cream, which won't break or curdle during the baking.

Going International
Two teaspoons of sweet paprika gives the casserole a Hungarian flare. One teaspoon of caraway seeds gives it a taste reminiscent of German casseroles. And increasing the mustard to 2 teaspoons and adding 1 tablespoon chopped fresh tarragon makes it decidedly French. Add any of these additional spices to the pan with the sour cream.

CHICKEN POT PIE 🍷🍷

makes a 1-quart casserole or two 2-cup servings

Remember frozen chicken pot pies? Some of us probably ate them on the nights our parents went out, or maybe for Sunday supper: that flaky crust, the rich chicken stew inside. Okay, it's better in memory, no doubt. But one thing's for sure: chicken pot pies are great when they're made from scratch, with a buttery biscuit topping and the chicken simmered in a creamy sauce. You can make this dish in either a shallow 1-quart casserole dish or in two 2-cup ramekins for individual servings.

4 chicken thighs (about
   ¾ pound total)
1 cup water
5 tablespoons unsalted butter
   (see Note)
1 small onion, chopped
2 medium carrots, chopped
2 medium celery ribs, minced
1 small garlic clove, minced
⅔ cup plus 1 tablespoon all-
   purpose flour
½ cup milk (regular, low-fat,
   or nonfat), or ½ cup heavy
   cream

¾ teaspoon salt
1 teaspoon minced fresh sage,
   or ½ teaspoon rubbed sage
½ teaspoon minced fresh
   thyme, or ¼ teaspoon dried
   thyme
¼ teaspoon freshly ground
   black pepper
¼ cup fresh peas, or ¼ cup
   frozen peas, thawed
2 tablespoons (or more) ice
   water

1. Place the chicken thighs in a small saucepan, cover with the water, then bring to a boil over high heat. Cover the pan, reduce the heat to low, and simmer for 15 minutes. Position the rack in the center of the oven and preheat the oven to 350°F.

2. Remove the chicken thighs from the saucepan. Skim the cooking liquid of any visible fat and impurities. Bring to a boil again over high heat, then continue boiling undisturbed for about 3 minutes, or until the liquid is reduced to ½ cup. If there are any impurities again on the surface, carefully skim them off, then set the reduced cooking liquid aside. Skin the chicken thighs, debone them, and roughly chop the meat. Set aside.

3. Melt 2 tablespoons of the butter in a medium saucepan set over medium heat. Add the onion, carrots, celery, and garlic. Cook for 5 minutes, or until the carrots soften and the onion is very fragrant, stirring frequently. Sprinkle 1 tablespoon of flour evenly over the vegetables. Cook for an additional 30 seconds undisturbed.

4. Whisk in the reduced ½ cup cooking liquid in a thin stream; continue whisking over medium heat for about 30 seconds, or until the mixture thickens. Whisk in the milk, ½ teaspoon of the salt, the sage, thyme, and pepper; cook for 30 seconds, whisking constantly. Stir in the chicken meat and peas. Divide this mixture between two 2-cup ramekins, or place in a shallow 1-quart casserole dish. Set aside while you prepare the biscuit topping.

5. Mix the remaining ⅔ cup of the flour and the remaining ¼ teaspoon salt in a small bowl. Cut in the remaining 3 tablespoons of the butter with a pastry cutter or with two forks until the mixture resembles coarse meal. Stir in 2 tablespoons ice water with a fork; continue stirring until a dough forms. You may need to add more ice water, depending on the day's humidity and the flour's density. If more ice water is needed, add it in ¼ teaspoon increments, stirring thoroughly with a fork until a soft dough forms. Drop this dough by tablespoonfuls onto the chicken mixture in the ramekins or in the casserole, covering as much of the surface as possible.

6. Bake for 35 minutes, or until the biscuit topping is brown and the chicken mixture is bubbling. Let stand at room temperature for 5 minutes before serving.

NOTE: The 2 tablespoons of the butter for cooking the vegetables can be at room temperature, but the remaining 3 tablespoons of the butter used in the biscuit topping must be very cold, right out of the refrigerator.

Rolling Out the Biscuit Topping

For a fancier presentation, you can roll out the biscuit topping. To do so, you'll need to make the dough before the chicken filling. First, prepare the biscuit dough as directed in the recipe, then wrap it tightly in plastic wrap and place it in the refrigerator for at least 20 minutes to chill. Meanwhile, prepare the chicken filling. Afterward, unwrap the dough and place it on a well-dusted work surface. Use a heavy rolling pin to roll it out to either an oval for the two ramekins or a top designed to fit exactly over the casserole dish. As you roll, do not press down into the dough; simply allow the weight of the rolling pin to roll out the dough. If using ramekins, cut the dough to fit each as a cover. If using a casserole dish, crimp the edges to make it fit inside the dish. Bake the casserole as directed.

STOVETOP CHICKEN AND RICE CASSEROLE

makes **2 servings**

In this simple meal of chicken, mushrooms, and wine, we've found that dried porcinis give the dish a more luxurious taste, even when the casserole's made in a small batch. Substitute dried chanterelles for a less aromatic, more subtle dish; or dried black trumpets for a more assertive, slightly sweet mushroom flavor. If you have a white wine you'd like to serve with dinner, use ⅓ cup in the dish, rather than the vermouth.

½ cup dried porcini
   (see page 9)
1 cup boiling water
2 bone-in chicken breast halves
   (about 16 ounces total)
¼ teaspoon salt
¼ teaspoon freshly ground
   black pepper
1 tablespoon unsalted butter,
   at room temperature

1 tablespoon olive oil
1 large shallot, minced
1 small garlic clove, minced
⅓ cup dry vermouth, or more
   as necessary
1 bay leaf
¼ cup plus 2 tablespoons
   white rice

1. Place the dried porcinis in a small bowl and stir in the boiling water. Let stand for 20 minutes, or until the mushrooms are pliable and quite fragrant. Meanwhile, season the chicken breasts with salt and pepper and set aside.

2. Melt the butter with the olive oil in a 10-inch skillet, preferably cast-iron, or a 10-inch sauté pan set over medium heat. Add the chicken breasts skin side down and cook for 3 minutes. Turn, sprinkle the shallot into the pan between the chicken pieces, and cook for about 2 more minutes, or until the shallot softens. Sprinkle the garlic into the spaces between the chicken pieces and cook for 10 seconds before pouring in the vermouth and tucking the bay leaf into the sauce. Bring the mixture to a boil, scraping up any browned bits on the bottom of the pan. Continue cooking for about 2 minutes, or until the wine is reduced to a glaze.

3. Add the rice to the pan (do not let any grains rest on the chicken breasts), then pour in the mushrooms and their soaking liquid. (If desired, strain the liquid for any sand. Better mushroom varieties are less sandy, but still may include a few grains.) Shake the pan to distribute the rice evenly in the broth, then bring the mixture to a boil over medium-high heat. Cover, reduce the heat to low, and simmer for about 18 minutes, or until the rice is tender. You may check the pan occasionally to make sure the rice isn't sticking. If it is, stir, reduce the heat even further, and add 1 or 2 tablespoons of vermouth to the pan. Remove the pan from the heat and let it stand covered for 5 minutes before serving.

ARROZ CON POLLO ⏱

makes **2 servings**

Why deny yourself this Spanish casserole of chicken, sausage, rice, and shellfish just because you're cooking for two? Better yet, it can be simplified somewhat to make it a quick, weekday meal using boneless chicken thighs (instead of a whole cut-up chicken) and shrimp (instead of clams or mussels). Keep the heat low so the rice doesn't stick.

1 tablespoon olive oil

⅓ pound chorizo, preferably Spanish chorizo, cut into ½-inch rings (see Note)

2 boneless, skinless chicken thighs (about ⅓ pound total)

1 small onion, finely chopped

1 medium garlic clove, minced

1 teaspoon chopped fresh rosemary, or ½ teaspoon chopped dried rosemary

1 teaspoon chopped fresh oregano, or ½ teaspoon dried oregano

½ teaspoon freshly ground black pepper

⅛ teaspoon saffron threads (see page 13)

One 14½-ounce can diced tomatoes

¼ cup plus 1 tablespoon long-grain white rice

6 medium shrimp (30 to 35 per pound), peeled and deveined

½ cup fresh shelled peas, or ½ cup frozen peas, thawed

1. Heat a 10- or 12-inch skillet over medium heat. Swirl in the oil, then add the chorizo. Cook for 3 minutes, stirring frequently, until browned. Using a slotted spoon, transfer the sausage to a plate lined with paper towels to drain; do not toss out the pan drippings.

2. Return the skillet to medium heat and cook the chicken thighs in the pan drippings for about 6 minutes, until browned, turning once. Transfer them to the plate with the sausages. Again, do not remove any of the pan drippings from the skillet.

3. Stir in the onion and garlic. Cook for 3 minutes over medium heat, or until translucent and very fragrant, stirring frequently. Crumble in the rosemary, oregano, pepper, and saffron, then stir in the tomatoes and rice. Nestle the sausage pieces and chicken thighs into the rice mixture. Cover, reduce the heat to low, and cook for about 20 minutes, or until the rice is tender.

4. Stir in the shrimp, cover, and cook for 1 minute. Remove the skillet from the heat and stir in the peas. Keep covered and let stand for 5 minutes before serving.

> NOTE: Chorizo is a Spanish or Mexican sausage. The widely available Mexican version is raw and needs to be cooked thoroughly; the Spanish version is smoked and needs only to be warmed up. Use either in this dish. Because the chorizo and the canned tomatoes are loaded with salt, there's no additional salt in the dish; but you can add a little more to taste, if you wish.

COQ AU VIN 🧳

Coq au vin is traditionally a two-day affair of marinating chicken in
wine, then slowly building a stew with layered flavors. Wonderful, yes,
if not exactly everyday cooking, whether made for two or twenty. But
streamlined somewhat, it's still soothing and delicious—here, a
deeply-flavored stew of chicken quarters and bacon cooked in red
wine. Serve this casserole on a bed of mashed potatoes, mashed acorn
squash, a scoop of white rice, or egg noodles. Use half of a standard
750-ml bottle of wine, preferably a dark Rhône bottling like a
Gigondas, for the chicken, and drink the rest with dinner; or buy a
"split" of red wine, a 375-ml bottle, and use all of it in this dish.

3 slices smoked bacon, cut into
 ½-inch pieces
2 chicken leg quarters (about
 1¼ pounds total)
1 small onion, minced
1 small garlic clove, minced
2 teaspoons all-purpose flour
½ bottle dry red wine
2 teaspoons fresh thyme, or
 1 teaspoon dried
 thyme
1 teaspoon minced fresh
 rosemary, or ½ teaspoon
 minced dried rosemary
¼ teaspoon celery seeds
1 bay leaf
1 tablespoon unsalted butter
8 ounces white button or
 cremini mushrooms,
 cleaned and sliced
2 tablespoons Grand Marnier
 or brandy

1. Heat a 3-quart Dutch oven or 3-quart pot over medium heat. Add
the bacon and fry about 5 minutes, or until very crisp, turning a few
times. Using a slotted spoon, transfer the bacon to a paper towel–lined
plate, reserving the rendered fat in the pot.

2. With the pot still over medium heat, add the chicken and brown it
for 6 minutes, turning once. You may need to shake the pan vigorously
or nudge the chicken pieces around the pan to keep them from sticking. Remove the chicken to the plate with the bacon. Do not remove
any of the pan drippings; maintain the heat under the pot.

3. Add the onion and garlic; cook for just 1 minute, stirring constantly, then stir in the flour, incorporating it thoroughly into the fat in the pan. Continue cooking for about 2 minutes, or until the flour begins to brown, stirring constantly.

4. Raise the heat to medium-high and pour in the wine, scraping up any browned bits on the bottom of the pan. Bring the mixture to a boil and boil for about 1 minute, or until the wine is reduced and somewhat thickened. Return the bacon, chicken pieces, and any accumulated juices to the pot. Stir in the thyme, rosemary, celery seed, and bay leaf. Cover, reduce the heat to low, and simmer for 30 minutes.

5. Meanwhile, melt the butter in a medium skillet or sauté pan set over medium heat. Add the mushrooms; cook for 4 minutes, or until they give off their liquid, stirring occasionally.

6. Carefully add the Grand Marnier or brandy to the skillet with the mushrooms. Stand back—the alcohol can ignite. (If it does, cover the skillet and remove it from the heat for 20 seconds to put the flames out.) Continue cooking for about 3 additional minutes, scraping up any browned bits in the pan, until the liquid reduces to a glaze. Cover and set aside off the heat.

7. After the chicken has cooked for 30 minutes, stir the cooked mushrooms and any of their pan juices into the pot. Cover and cook for 10 minutes. Uncover and cook for about 5 more minutes, to thicken somewhat. Serve immediately.

Jelly, Anyone?
Coq au vin is often finished with a little red currant jelly, melted into the stew for the last 10 minutes of cooking. It gives the dish a sweet, slightly sour taste, very authentic and quite good. If you choose this traditional finish for the casserole, use only brandy, not the far sweeter Grand Marnier, to deglaze the pan with the mushrooms.

POTATO *and* SPINACH CASSEROLE 💼

makes a 1-quart casserole

In this vegetarian casserole, thin potato slices are used like wide flat noodles, separating the layers of creamy spinach.

2 tablespoons unsalted butter, plus additional for buttering the casserole dish

1 large Russet potato (about ¾ pound)

1 small onion, chopped

One 10-ounce package frozen chopped spinach, thawed and squeezed of all excess water

2 large eggs, at room temperature

½ cup crumbled feta (about 2 ounces)

2 tablespoons chopped fresh dill, or 1 tablespoon dried dill

2 tablespoons chopped fresh parsley, or 2 teaspoons dried parsley

½ teaspoon freshly ground black pepper

¼ teaspoon ground cinnamon

¼ teaspoon salt

1. Position the rack in the center of the oven and preheat the oven to 350°F. Butter a shallow 1-quart casserole dish and set it aside.

2. Fill a large bowl with water. Peel the potato and cut it in half lengthwise. Use a vegetable peeler to make long, thin strips, like noodles, from the cut side of the potato, letting the strips fall into the water as they are sliced off.

3. Bring a medium pot of water to a boil over high heat. Drain the potato slices, blot them dry with paper towels, then boil the slices for 2 minutes, or just until they lose their raw, crunchy feel but not until they are cooked through. Drain, refresh with cold water, then set aside.

4. Melt 1 tablespoon of the butter in a small skillet or sauté pan set over low heat. Add the onion and soften for about 4 minutes, or until golden, stirring frequently. Cool for 5 minutes off the heat.

5. Scrape the onions and any butter left in the pan into a food processor fitted with the chopping blade or into a large blender. Add the spinach, eggs, feta, dill, parsley, pepper, cinnamon, and salt. Pulse six or seven times, until the mixture is smooth, scraping down the sides of the bowl as necessary. Alternatively, place all the ingredients in a large bowl and whisk them until smooth. This hand-whisked mixture will not be as creamy as the one from a food processor.

6. Now build the casserole. Divide the potato slices into four equal portions. Use one-fourth to cover the bottom of the casserole, overlapping the slices as necessary to create a solid layer. Top with one-third of the spinach mixture. Then use another quarter of the potato slices to create another layer. Top this with half the remaining spinach mixture. Make a third layer of potatoes, then top with the remaining spinach mixture. Finally, top with the remaining potato slices.

7. Melt the remaining 1 tablespoon of butter in a small saucepan set over low heat or in a small dish in the microwave on high for 20 seconds. Pour the melted butter over the casserole, then bake for 40 minutes, or until bubbly and lightly browned. Let stand for 5 minutes at room temperature before serving.

More Texture, More Crunch
Stir 2 tablespoons of any of the following into the spinach mixture before layering it in the casserole dish: chopped roasted chickpeas, golden raisins, sliced blanched almonds, toasted pepitás, toasted pine nuts.

No-Fry
Eggplant Parmesan 💼

makes 2 servings

We love eggplant parmesan, but we're the first to admit it can sometimes be a greasy mess. So we set about to make a lighter, healthier dish. Here, the eggplant slices aren't fried; they're salted, drained, lightly coated with olive oil, and then baked before they're layered in the dish with cheese and an herbed tomato sauce.

2 small eggplants (sometimes called baby eggplants, about 7 ounces each), peeled and cut into ½-inch-thick slices
1 teaspoon salt
3 tablespoons olive oil
1 small onion, minced
1 large garlic clove, minced
1 teaspoon chopped fresh oregano, or ½ teaspoon dried oregano
1 teaspoon chopped fresh basil, or ½ teaspoon dried basil
¼ teaspoon freshly ground black pepper
One 14½-ounce can diced tomatoes
2 ounces Parmigiano-Reggiano, shaved (see Note)
¼ teaspoon grated nutmeg

1. Sprinkle the eggplant slices with ½ teaspoon of the salt. Stack them vertically in a colander, or lay them out on paper towels to drain. If they're laid on paper towels, they should be turned once while draining. Let stand for 30 minutes, then blot dry with clean paper towels. Meanwhile, position the rack in the center of the oven and preheat the oven to 400°F.

2. Rub 2 tablespoons of the olive oil into the eggplant slices, place them on a lipped baking sheet to catch any drips, and bake for 15 minutes. Turn and bake for about 15 additional minutes, or until lightly browned. Remove from the oven and set aside; reduce the oven temperature to 350°F.

3. Heat a medium skillet or sauté pan over medium heat. Swirl in the remaining 1 tablespoon of olive oil, then add the onion and soften for 2 minutes, stirring frequently. Stir in the garlic, oregano, basil, pepper, and the remaining ½ teaspoon salt. Cook for 30 seconds, stirring constantly; then raise the heat to medium-high, pour in the tomatoes with their juice, and bring the sauce to a simmer. Cover, reduce the heat to low, and simmer for 20 minutes, until thickened. The dish can be made in advance up to this point. Cover the eggplant slices and the sauce and refrigerate separately for up to 24 hours; allow both to come back to room temperature before proceeding with the dish.

4. Layer the following in this order in a 6-cup casserole dish or an 8-inch square baking pan: one-third of the tomato sauce, half the eggplant slices, half the cheese slices, ⅛ teaspoon grated nutmeg, half of the remaining tomato sauce, the remaining eggplant slices, the remaining cheese shavings, and the remaining ⅛ teaspoon grated nutmeg. Top with the remaining tomato sauce. You may have to cut the eggplant slices to make them fit in one layer, or you may have to overlap them a bit.

5. Bake for 30 minutes, or until thickened and bubbly. Let stand at room temperature for 5 minutes before serving.

> **N O T E :** Shave the cheese with a cheese plane, a tool found in most grocery stores or kitchenware outlets, or a sturdy vegetable peeler. Simply drag it across the hard cheese, creating paper-thin slices that you can layer in the final casserole. Alternatively, grate the cheese with the large holes of a box grater or in a food processor fitted with the grating blade. The final dish will not be as gooey as one with shaved cheese.

STUFFED BAKED POTATOES, THREE WAYS ⏱

makes **2 stuffed baked potatoes**

These are really just little individual casseroles: the potato skins crunchy, the filling moist and creamy. Use only baking potatoes, preferably Russets, for these recipes.

WITH SHRIMP, FETA, AND DILL

These garlicky twice-baked potatoes have a Greek twist. They're surprisingly light, the perfect dinner for any night of the week.

2 large baking potatoes, preferably Russets (about ¾ pound each), scrubbed
1 tablespoon olive oil, plus 2 teaspoons more for garnish, if desired
1 large garlic clove, minced
⅓ pound medium shrimp (about 30 per pound), peeled, deveined, and roughly chopped
⅓ cup plain yogurt (regular, low-fat, or nonfat)

¼ cup crumbled feta (about 2 ounces)
2 tablespoons chopped black pitted olives
2 tablespoons chopped fresh dill, or 1 tablespoon dried dill
¼ teaspoon salt, or to taste
¼ teaspoon freshly ground black pepper

1. Position the oven rack in the middle of the oven and preheat the oven to 375°F. Puncture each potato in three or four places, then microwave on high until soft for anywhere from 7 to 10 minutes, depending on your microwave's power and the potato's size. Remove to a wire rack and cool for 5 minutes. Alternatively, place the potatoes on a baking sheet and bake until soft, about 1 hour and 5 minutes.

2. Heat a medium skillet or sauté pan over medium heat. Swirl in the oil, then add the garlic and cook for 1 minute, or just until fragrant. Add the shrimp and cook for 2 minutes, or until pink and firm, stirring often. Transfer the contents of the pan to a medium bowl (see Note). Stir in the yogurt, feta, olives, dill, salt, and pepper until well combined.

3. When the potatoes are cool enough to handle, slice the top third off each potato lengthwise. Use a small spoon to scoop the inside flesh of the larger sections into a second medium bowl. Leave ⅛ inch of potato flesh against the skin so that it will not collapse when stuffed. Scoop the insides of the cut-off top sections into the bowl as well; discard the top skins. Use a potato masher or a wooden spoon to mix these ingredients until soft and uniform, about 30 seconds. Alternatively, you can mash the potatoes with an electric mixer at low speed until creamy. Stir in the prepared shrimp mixture.

4. Place the large potato-skin shells in a shallow 1-quart casserole dish; divide the mashed potato mixture between them, mounding it with a spoon. If desired, drizzle 1 teaspoon olive oil over the top of each potato. Bake for 15 minutes, or until the stuffing is steaming hot. Serve immediately.

> N O T E : You can skip the step of sautéing the shrimp and garlic by substituting ⅓ pound precooked cocktail shrimp, peeled and roughly chopped, and ¼ teaspoon garlic powder. Add these and the olive oil to the bowl with the yogurt and other ingredients.

WITH ZUCCHINI, GOAT CHEESE, AND WALNUTS

This vegetarian casserole has a California twist, with soft goat cheese and walnuts. You can substitute a hard, aged goat cheese for a more pungent taste; grate an equivalent amount directly into the mashed potato mixture.

2 large baking potatoes, preferably Russets (about ¾ pound each), scrubbed

2 tablespoons olive oil

1 large garlic clove, minced

1 medium zucchini (about 5 ounces), cut into ½-inch dice

¼ cup heavy cream, or ¼ cup half-and-half

¼ teaspoon red pepper flakes

¼ teaspoon salt, or to taste

¼ teaspoon freshly ground black pepper

¼ cup fresh goat cheese, such as Montrachet (about 2 ounces), crumbled

3 tablespoons chopped walnut pieces

2 tablespoons grated Parmigiano-Reggiano (about ½ ounce)

1. Position the oven rack in the middle of the oven and preheat the oven to 375°F. Puncture each potato in three or four places, then microwave on high until soft for anywhere from 7 to 10 minutes, depending on your microwave's power and the potato's size. Remove to a wire rack and cool for 5 minutes. Alternatively, place the potatoes on a baking sheet and bake until soft, about 1 hour and 5 minutes.

2. Heat a medium skillet or sauté pan over medium-low heat. Swirl in the oil, reduce the heat to low, then add the garlic and cook slowly for 3 minutes to flavor the oil, stirring occasionally. Do not let the garlic brown; if it does, reduce the heat even further. Once the garlic is very aromatic, raise the heat to medium and add the zucchini. Stir-fry for about 2 minutes, or until softened. Set aside off the heat while you prepare the potatoes.

3. When they are cool enough to handle, slice the top third off each potato lengthwise. Use a small spoon to scoop the inside flesh of the larger sections into a medium bowl. Leave ⅛-inch of potato flesh against the skin so that it will not collapse when stuffed. Scoop the insides of the cut-off top sections into the bowl as well; discard the top skins. Use a potato masher, a wooden spoon, or an electric mixer at medium speed to mash the potatoes for about 30 seconds. Add the cream, red pepper flakes, salt, and pepper and continue beating until the mixture is smooth and uniform. Use a wooden spoon to stir in the goat cheese, walnuts, and the contents of the pan with the zucchini; continue stirring until all is well combined.

4. Place the hollowed-out potato skins in a shallow 1-quart casserole dish; divide the mashed potato mixture between them, mounding it with a spoon. Sprinkle 1 tablespoon grated Parmigiano-Reggiano over each potato. Bake for 15 minutes, or until the cheese is browned and the stuffing is heated through. Serve immediately.

AU CROQUE MONSIEUR
(WITH HAM AND GRUYÈRE)

A croque monsieur is French diner food: an open-faced grilled ham and cheese sandwich. We've taken those tastes and put them in a stuffed baked potato for a quick but hearty weeknight meal. Canadian bacon is basically smoked pork loin; have your butcher slice it thick for you, so you can cut it into thick cubes to add to the potatoes.

2 large baking potatoes, preferably Russets (about ¾ pound each), scrubbed
2 tablespoons unsalted butter
1 large leek, white part only, cleaned of any sand and roughly chopped
¼ pound Canadian bacon, roughly chopped
¼ cup heavy cream

¼ teaspoon salt, or to taste
¼ teaspoon freshly ground black pepper
½ cup grated Gruyère (about 2 ounces)
1 teaspoon fresh thyme, or ½ teaspoon dried thyme

1. Position the oven rack in the middle of the oven and preheat the oven to 375°F. Puncture each potato in three or four places, then microwave on high until soft for anywhere from 7 to 10 minutes, depending on your microwave's power and the potato's size. Remove to a wire rack and cool for 5 minutes. Alternatively, place the potatoes on a baking sheet and bake until soft, about 1 hour and 5 minutes.

2. Melt the butter in a medium skillet or sauté pan over medium heat. Add the leek and cook for 2 minutes, or until soft, stirring occasionally. Add the Canadian bacon and sauté for about 1 minute, or just until warmed through. Remove the pan from the heat and set aside while you prepare the potatoes.

3. When they are cool enough to handle, slice the top third off each potato lengthwise. Use a small spoon to scoop the inside flesh of the larger sections into a medium bowl. Leave ⅛ inch of potato flesh against the skin so that it will not collapse when stuffed. Scoop the insides of the cut-off top sections into the bowl as well; discard the top skins. Use a potato masher, a wooden spoon, or an electric mixer at medium speed to mash the potatoes for about 30 seconds. Add the cream, salt, and pepper; continue beating until the mixture is light and fluffy. Using a wooden spoon, mix in ¼ cup of the grated cheese, the thyme, and the contents of the pan with the leeks and the Canadian bacon. Stir until smooth.

4. Place the large potato-skin shells in a shallow 1-quart casserole dish; divide the mashed potato mixture between them, mounding it with a spoon. Sprinkle 2 tablespoons of grated cheese over each potato. Bake for 15 minutes, or until the cheese is browned and bubbling. Serve at once.

Pastas

Pasta dishes are perfect for small-batch cooking: open a small can of diced tomatoes, add a few vegetables and some cooked pasta, and dinner's ready in minutes. In all cases, make the noodles before you make the sauce, because it will be done long before they are, if everything's started at the same time. There's also no reason to be fussy about pasta. Although we always call for a specific shape, use what you have on hand—with the exception of lasagna noodles or cannelloni tubes, of course! You won't use the whole box or bag with any of these dishes: just 6 ounces of dried pasta in most cases. The rest will keep for months in your pantry, ready for the next time you want to make a simple but satisfying pasta dish after a busy day.

PASTA BOLOGNESE

makes **2 servings**

"**B**olognese," of course, just refers to any dish from Bologna, Italy—but it has come to mean a thick ragoût of ground meat, vegetables, and tomatoes, served over flat noodles such as fettuccine. The traditional preparation, while exquisite, takes hours to make: a slow-simmering, all-day task, and not exactly everyday fare for a busy cook. Fortunately, small batches cook faster than larger ones, and canned diced tomatoes speed up the process even more.

2 tablespoons olive oil
1 large shallot, minced
1 small carrot, minced
1 small celery rib, minced
1 large garlic clove, minced
⅓ pound ground veal, or lean ground beef
⅓ cup milk (regular, low-fat, or nonfat)
One 14½-ounce can diced tomatoes
1½ teaspoons chopped fresh oregano, or ½ teaspoon dried oregano

1 teaspoon fresh thyme, or ½ teaspoon dried thyme
½ teaspoon salt
¼ teaspoon freshly ground black pepper
¼ teaspoon grated nutmeg
6 ounces dried fettuccine or other flat noodles, cooked according to package instructions
2 tablespoons grated Parmigiano-Reggiano (about ½ ounce)

1. Heat a medium saucepan or sauté pan over medium heat. Swirl in the oil, then stir in the shallot, carrot, celery, and garlic. Cook for about 4 minutes, or until the carrots soften and the shallot is very aromatic, stirring occasionally.

2. Crumble in the ground meat and cook for only 30 seconds, just until it has lost its raw, red color, stirring constantly but taking care not to break up the meat fibers. Pour in the milk and cook for 2 more minutes, or until it's almost evaporated, stirring often. Now stir in the tomatoes (with their juice), the oregano, thyme, salt, pepper, and nutmeg. Bring the mixture to a boil, reduce the heat to low, and simmer uncovered for 20 minutes, or until thickened, stirring occasionally.

3. Stir in the cooked pasta and cook for 1 minute to heat through. Divide between two bowls, top each with 1 tablespoon of the grated cheese, and serve.

LINGUINE WITH SAGE PESTO

makes **2 servings**

Traditionally, pesto is a fresh, uncooked sauce made with basil, cheese, pine nuts, and olive oil; but here's an autumnal variation made with sage and parsley, best served over thin noodles such as fettuccine. Of course, you needn't wait until the fall to have this dish. Dried herbs won't work here—the leaf varieties won't blend smoothly, and rubbed sage will overpower the sauce.

½ cup packed fresh parsley, preferably flat-leaf parsley

2 tablespoons packed fresh sage leaves

2 tablespoons freshly grated Parmigiano-Reggiano (about ½ ounce)

1 tablespoon chopped walnuts

1 small garlic clove, halved

¼ teaspoon freshly ground black pepper

⅓ cup plus 1 tablespoon olive oil, preferably extra-virgin olive oil

6 ounces dried fettuccine, or other wide noodles, cooked according to package instructions

1 teaspoon grated lemon zest

1. Place the parsley, sage, Parmigiano-Reggiano, walnut pieces, garlic, and pepper in a food processor fitted with the chopping blade, or in a mini food processor, or a wide blender. Pulse four or five times until coarsely chopped, scraping down the sides of the bowl as necessary. With the food processor or blender running, drizzle in the olive oil until a thick sauce forms. (The consistency of pesto is a matter of preference. If you prefer a coarser sauce, pulse only a couple of times before you add the oil, just to chop everything roughly. For a smoother pesto, pulse up to ten times before you add the oil.)

2. Toss the cooked pasta with the sage pesto in a large bowl, sprinkle with the grated lemon zest, and serve immediately.

SPAGHETTI WITH CLAMS

makes **2 servings**

This garlicky pasta dish is reminiscent of one commonly served in working-class Venetian restaurants. Use the clams the day you buy them: scrub them to remove any sand on their shells, then place them in a bowl in the refrigerator, under damp paper towels, until you're ready to use them. Don't cook any that refuse to close when tapped, and don't eat any that remain closed after cooking. If you prefer, substitute white wine for the vermouth, using something you'd like to drink with dinner.

¼ cup olive oil

4 medium garlic cloves, finely minced

½ teaspoon red pepper flakes

2 ounces pancetta (see page 10), roughly chopped

½ cup dry vermouth

1 pound small clams, such as littlenecks or Pismos, scrubbed (see headnote)

6 ounces dried spaghetti, cooked according to package instructions

1 cup chopped arugula

2 tablespoons freshly grated Parmigiano-Reggiano (about ½ ounce)

1 tablespoon unsalted butter

1. Heat a large saucepan over medium heat. Pour in the olive oil, then toss in the garlic and red pepper flakes. Cook for just 10 seconds, stirring constantly. Be careful—the oils in the pepper flakes will volatilize and can burn your eyes. Stir in the pancetta and cook for about 3 minutes, or until lightly browned and frizzled at the edges, stirring often so the garlic doesn't burn.

2. Pour in the vermouth and scrape up any browned bits on the bottom of the pan. Bring the mixture to a boil, add the clams, cover the pan, and simmer for 5 minutes, just until they open.

3. Stir in the spaghetti, arugula, cheese, and butter. Toss to coat, cook for an additional 30 seconds to heat through and wilt the greens, and serve at once.

FUSILLI AND MEATBALLS

makes **2 generous servings**

No wonder this is a classic: meatballs, a simple tomato sauce, and pasta. It's rich, satisfying, and not all that hard to make. Best of all, this time it's just for two. Peas may be a bit of a surprise here, but they add a nice green "summeriness" to this hearty dish. Of course, to make this even more classic, substitute spaghetti or linguine for the fusilli.

½ pound lean ground beef, preferably ground sirloin

¼ cup plus 2 tablespoons plain dried bread crumbs

3 tablespoons chopped fresh parsley, or 1 tablespoon dried parsley

2 tablespoons freshly grated Parmigiano-Reggiano (about ½ ounce)

1½ teaspoons minced fresh sage, or ½ teaspoon rubbed sage

2 tablespoons milk (regular, low-fat, or nonfat)

2 small garlic cloves, minced

1 large egg, separated, at room temperature

¼ teaspoon salt

¼ teaspoon freshly ground black pepper

2 tablespoons olive oil

1 small onion, minced

1 medium carrot, minced

1 medium celery rib, minced

1 ounce pancetta (see page 10), finely chopped

One 14½-ounce can diced tomatoes

½ cup dry vermouth

2 teaspoons minced fresh oregano, or 1 teaspoon dried oregano

1 teaspoon sugar

½ teaspoon red pepper flakes

½ cup fresh peas, or ½ cup frozen peas, defrosted

6 ounces dried fusilli or ziti, or 6 ounces dried spaghetti, cooked according to package instructions

1. Mix the ground beef, 2 tablespoons of the bread crumbs, 1 table-spoon fresh or 1 teaspoon dried parsley, the cheese, sage, milk, half the garlic, the egg yolk, salt, and pepper in a medium bowl with a fork, just until combined. Use your hands or a wooden spoon so as not to overwork the mixture, and tear the meat fibers. Shape this mixture into 8 meatballs, each about the size of a golf ball.

2. Beat the egg white in a small bowl until frothy. Place the remaining ¼ cup bread crumbs on a cutting board or a clean, dry work surface.

3. Heat a large saucepan over medium heat and swirl in the olive oil. Dip a meatball first in the beaten egg white, then roll it in the bread crumbs, and finally place it in the skillet. Repeat with the remaining meatballs. Fry them for about 3 minutes, or until lightly browned all over but not until cooked through, turning occasionally. Using a slotted spoon, transfer them to a plate lined with paper towels to drain, but do not drain the pan drippings from the skillet.

4. Stir in the onion, carrot, and celery and cook over medium heat for about 3 minutes, or until soft and fragrant, stirring occasionally. Stir in the chopped pancetta and the remaining garlic, then cook for 2 more minutes, or until the pancetta is lightly browned, stirring frequently.

5. Pour in the tomatoes (with their juice) and the vermouth, stir well, then add the oregano, sugar, pepper flakes, the remaining parsley, and the meatballs. Cover the pan, reduce the heat to low, and simmer for 15 minutes, stirring once or twice. Stir in the peas and simmer, uncovered, for about 5 more minutes, or until the sauce thickens somewhat.

6. Add the pasta and toss to coat. Cook for 1 additional minute to heat through, then divide between two bowls and serve.

SPAGHETTI *with* EGGPLANT, BELL PEPPER, *and* GOAT CHEESE

makes **2 servings**

This is a simplified, everyday take on an Italian favorite of fried eggplant simmered in a tomato ragoût. Ours is less oily because the eggplant slices are baked, not fried. It's also quicker to make. Soft, mellow goat cheese stands in for the long-simmered ragoût—it thickens the sauce, giving it a creamy richness in no time. That convenience comes with one caveat: because the sauce cooks so quickly, use only fresh basil, not dried, which will not have enough time to soften and release its flavor.

1 small eggplant (about ½ pound), preferably white, peeled and cut into ½-inch rounds

2½ tablespoons olive oil

1 small onion, chopped

1 small yellow or red bell pepper, cored, seeded, and thinly sliced into rings

2 medium garlic cloves, minced

2 Italian plum tomatoes, chopped (a little less than 1 cup)

¼ cup packed fresh basil leaves, shredded

¼ teaspoon salt

¼ teaspoon pepper

6 ounces dried spaghetti, linguine, or fettuccine, cooked in unsalted water according to package directions, ⅓ cup cooking water reserved (see Note)

2 ounces fresh goat cheese, such as Montrachet, at room temperature

1. Preheat the oven to 375°F. Rub the eggplant slices with 1 tablespoon of the olive oil and place them on a large lipped baking sheet. Bake for 10 minutes, turn, then bake for about 10 more minutes, or until lightly browned and softened but not mushy. Remove the pan from the oven, cool the slices on the baking sheet for 10 minutes, then slice them into thin strips. Set aside.

2. Heat a large skillet or sauté pan over medium heat. Swirl in the remaining 1½ tablespoons olive oil, then toss in the onion, bell pepper, and garlic. Cook and stir for 3 minutes, or until the pepper is pliable and the garlic is only lightly browned. Stir in the chopped tomatoes and the eggplant and cook for 2 more minutes, just until the tomatoes start to break down, stirring often.

3. Stir in the basil, salt, and pepper, then add the pasta and the reserved pasta cooking water. Toss well to heat through, then crumble the goat cheese over the dish. Divide between serving bowls and serve immediately.

> **NOTE:** Since some of the pasta cooking water is used to make the sauce, cook the noodles in unsalted water so as not to overpower the sauce with salt.

Spicing Things Up
Add zest to this dish with any or all of the following, stirred into the sauce with the basil:

2 teaspoons minced fresh oregano

½ teaspoon red pepper flakes

⅓ cup dry vermouth or white wine (in which case, omit the pasta cooking water)

SPAGHETTI WITH FRESH TOMATOES, PANCETTA, and SMOKED MOZZARELLA

makes **2 servings**

As with many quick-cooking pasta dishes, there's no substitute for the fresh basil here. Fortunately, many markets now sell fresh herbs in small bunches. If you can only buy a large bunch of basil, use any leftovers on sandwiches or in an omelet the next day. Any pasta will work, although spaghetti is the classic.

3 tablespoons olive oil

2 ounces pancetta (see page 10), roughly chopped

3 garlic cloves, slivered

4 medium Italian plum tomatoes, chopped (about 1¾ cups)

½ teaspoon salt

¼ teaspoon red pepper flakes

¼ cup packed fresh basil leaves, shredded

6 ounces dried spaghetti, cooked according to package instructions

3 ounces smoked mozzarella, cut into ¼-inch cubes

1. Heat a large skillet or sauté pan over medium heat. Swirl in the olive oil, then toss in the pancetta and cook for about 5 minutes, or until crispy, stirring occasionally. Add the garlic and cook for just 15 seconds, stirring constantly; stir in the tomatoes, salt, and red pepper flakes. Bring the mixture to a simmer, cover, reduce the heat to low, and cook for about 7 minutes, or until the tomatoes have broken down and made a sauce.

2. Stir in the shredded basil, immediately raise the heat to medium-high, and cook, uncovered, for 1 minute, or until the basil wilts and the mixture thickens slightly, stirring constantly.

3. Stir in the cooked spaghetti, remove the pan from the heat, and stir in the cheese. Cover the pan and let it stand at room temperature for 5 minutes so that the cheese melts. Toss, then serve.

ZITI *with* CURRY CARROT CREAM SAUCE

makes **2 servings**

Ready in minutes, this light cream-sauce pasta dish is a satisfying vegetarian supper. The curry powder gives it a new twist—the carrots, sweetness and depth. After you add the cream, let the sauce reduce until it coats the back of a wooden spoon without running off— dip a wooden spoon into the sauce, then run your finger through the sauce on the back of the spoon; the line you make should hold firm, not run.

1 tablespoon canola oil or other vegetable oil
1 cup shredded carrots (see Note)
2 teaspoons curry powder
1½ teaspoons peeled, minced fresh ginger
2 tablespoons dry vermouth

½ cup light or heavy cream
6 ounces dried ziti, cooked according to package instructions
2 tablespoons grated Asiago or freshly grated Parmigiano-Reggiano (about ½ ounce)
½ teaspoon salt, or to taste

1. Heat a large skillet or sauté pan over medium heat. Swirl in the oil, then stir in the shredded carrots and soften for 2 minutes, stirring frequently. Stir in the curry powder and ginger; cook for only about 20 seconds, until fragrant, then stir in the vermouth and cook for another 15 seconds, until bubbly, scraping up any spice grains that have adhered to the bottom of the pan. Stir in the cream and continue cooking for about 2 minutes, or just until the cream is thickened so that it coats the back of a wooden spoon.

2. Stir in the cooked ziti, the cheese, and salt. Cook for about 30 seconds, just until heated through, and serve.

N O T E : Shred the carrots with a vegetable peeler or a food processor fitted with a shredding blade. If desired, squeeze the shredded carrots between paper towels to release as much water as possible. This will make the final dish less "saucy."

103

LINGUINE NOGADA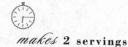

makes **2 servings**

Nogada is a traditional Mexican sauce of walnuts and cream. Although it's usually served over enchiladas, try it on pasta. Salt is optional here because of the cheese; add any additional salt sparingly. This vegetarian dish is best with a fresh fruit salad dressed with a raspberry vinaigrette or poppy seed dressing.

1 tablespoon unsalted butter

1 small onion, finely chopped

¾ cup walnuts, finely chopped

½ teaspoon ground cinnamon

⅛ teaspoon grated nutmeg

2 tablespoons dry vermouth

½ cup heavy cream

6 ounces dried linguine, cooked according to the package instructions

2 tablespoons grated queso blanco or Monterey Jack (about ½ ounce)

½ teaspoon salt, optional

1. Melt the butter in a medium skillet set over medium heat, then stir in the onion and walnuts. Cook for about 2 minutes, or until the onion is golden and the walnuts are lightly browned, stirring frequently.

2. Stir in the cinnamon, nutmeg, and vermouth. Cook for just 20 seconds, or until the spices are fragrant; stir in the cream. Bring the mixture back to a simmer and cook for about 2 minutes, or until the cream is thickened so that it coats the back of a wooden spoon, stirring frequently.

3. Stir in the cooked linguine, the cheese, and salt, if desired. Toss, then cook for just 20 seconds to heat through. Serve at once.

RICE NOODLES *with* DRIED PEARS *and* CHERRY TOMATOES

makes 2 **servings**

Many Asian recipes, as you know, suffer from a plethora of ingredients, a mile-long list that seems daunting. But that's actually the good news: the flavors are built and layered quickly with condiments, rather than long-simmered or slow-roasted. Some of those traditional condiments like nam pla and hoisin sauce are combined here with dried pears and ripe tomatoes to give the Asian-inspired noodle dish a subtle, tangy sweetness. Rice stick noodles, about ¼ inch wide and made from rice flour, are available in Asian markets and most gourmet stores. If you can't find them, substitute the much thinner mung bean noodles.

5 ounces rice stick noodles
  (see headnote)
3 tablespoons nam pla
  (see page 10)
2 tablespoons hoisin sauce
  (see Note)
1 tablespoon water
1 tablespoon packed light
  brown sugar
2 dashes Tabasco sauce, or to
  taste
1 tablespoon peanut oil
1 large shallot, minced
1 large garlic clove, minced

4 large dried pear slices, cut
  into thin strips
¾ cup snow peas (about
  2 ounces)
½ cup bean sprouts (about
  1 ounce)
10 cherry tomatoes, halved
2 tablespoons unsalted
  peanuts, chopped
2 tablespoons chopped fresh
  cilantro, or 2 teaspoons
  dried cilantro
1 tablespoon lime juice

1. Place the rice stick noodles in a large bowl or baking pan. Cover them with cool water and soak for 10 minutes.

2. Meanwhile, bring a medium saucepan filled halfway with water to a boil over high heat. Drain the noodles and stir them into the boiling water. Cook for 2 minutes, just until they are still firm to the bite. Drain and rinse well under cool water to keep from sticking. Set aside.

3. In a small bowl, whisk the nam pla, hoisin, water, brown sugar, and Tabasco sauce until the sugar has dissolved. Set aside.

4. Heat a wok or medium sauté pan over medium-high heat. Swirl in the oil, then add the shallot and garlic. Cook for 1 minute, just until the shallot softens. Do not let the garlic brown. Stir in the dried pears and snow peas; cook for 20 seconds, tossing and stirring constantly. Add the bean sprouts and tomatoes; cook for an additional 30 seconds.

5. Pour the reserved nam pla mixture into the pan. Stir to coat the vegetables, then add the reserved noodles. Cook for about 30 seconds, just until the sauce comes to a simmer and thickens slightly.

6. Remove the pan from the heat and stir in the peanuts, cilantro, and lime juice. Toss gently, then divide between two bowls and serve immediately.

> **NOTE:** Hoisin sauce is a Chinese condiment made from soybeans, garlic, vinegar, spices, and sweeteners. It's available in the Asian aisle of many supermarkets, and in all Asian markets. Look for a dark, thick, pastelike sauce, preferably one bottled in China. Tightly covered, it will keep for up to a year in the refrigerator.

Vegetarian Dishes

Long gone are the days when vegetarian meant boring. Today's vegetarian cooking is light but flavorful, healthy but satisfying. These recipes run the gamut from quick sandwiches to comforting baked dishes. Use the freshest produce you can find—be very picky about which bell peppers or potatoes you choose at the market. That way, the flavors permeate the dish without a lot of other fandango.

BARBECUE TOFU BURRITOS

makes **2 large burritos**

These gooey burritos are best eaten with a knife and fork. The sundried tomatoes should be dry but still pliable. If you use those packed in oil, drain and rinse them before adding them to the sauce.

2 tablespoons unsalted hulled pepitás (see page 11), or 2 tablespoons pecan pieces
One 15-ounce can pinto beans, drained and rinsed
¾ cup purchased barbecue sauce
¼ cup sundried tomatoes, chopped
2 tablespoons water

8 ounces firm tofu, drained and cut into ½-inch cubes
Two 12- to 14-inch flour tortillas, warmed (see page 69)
¼ cup shredded Monterey Jack cheese (about 2 ounces)
2 tablespoons chopped fresh cilantro

1. Toast the pepitás or nuts in a small, dry skillet set over low heat for 5 minutes, tossing them frequently until they brown. If using pepitás, they will pop as they toast. Remove them from the skillet and set aside.

2. Mix the beans, barbecue sauce, sundried tomatoes, and water in a small saucepan set over medium heat. Bring the mixture to a boil, cover, reduce the heat to low, and simmer for 10 minutes, stirring occasionally.

3. Add the tofu cubes to the sauce. Simmer for 10 additional minutes, stirring occasionally but carefully, so as not to break up the tofu.

4. Lay the two warmed tortillas on your work surface. Divide the barbecue sauce mixture between them, spooning it down the center. Divide the toasted nuts between the two tortillas, sprinkling them on top of the sauce. Top each with half the cheese and half the cilantro. Fold the tortillas closed and transfer to two plates. Serve at once.

RED COOKED TOFU

makes 2 servings

"Red cooked" is a Chinese technique of stewing meat or tofu in a soy sauce broth. With long cooking, aged soy sauce mellows and becomes woody, almost sweet. It also develops a deep red cast—thus, the name of the dish. Serve this vegetarian stew over white or brown rice or on top of cooked soba noodles.

20 dried shiitake mushrooms
1½ cups boiling water
3 tablespoons soy sauce, preferably dark soy sauce (see Note)
1½ tablespoon Shao Shing (see page 13)
1 teaspoon red chili paste (see page 12)
¾ teaspoon sugar
1½ tablespoons peanut oil
2 medium scallions, minced

1 medium carrot, peeled and minced
2 medium garlic cloves, minced
2 teaspoons peeled, minced fresh ginger
Vegetable oil for the steamer
8 ounces firm tofu, drained
1 teaspoon arrowroot or cornstarch
1 teaspoon water
1 teaspoon rice vinegar (see page 12)

1. Place the mushrooms in a medium bowl and cover with the boiling water. Set aside to soak for 20 minutes.

2. Skim off and reserve ¾ cup of the soaking liquid from the bowl. (The liquid may be sandy—if so, strain it through a colander lined with cheesecloth.) Drain the mushrooms and discard the remainder of the liquid. Stem the mushrooms, then clean the caps of any residual sand by running your fingers over the gills while holding the mushroom cap under running water. Thinly slice the caps and set them aside.

3. Whisk the reserved soaking liquid, soy sauce, Shao Shing, red chili paste, and sugar together in a small bowl until the sugar dissolves. Set aside.

4. Heat a medium saucepan over medium-high heat. Swirl in the peanut oil, then toss in the scallions, carrot, garlic, and ginger. Stir-fry for 1 minute, or just until the scallions soften. Pour in the soy sauce mixture, stir well, then bring the mixture to a simmer. Cover, reduce the heat to low, and simmer for 10 minutes.

5. Meanwhile, place the tofu and sliced mushroom caps in an oiled bamboo steamer set over a pot half full of simmering water, or in an oiled vegetable steamer set over 1 inch of simmering water. Cover and steam for 6 minutes. Remove the tofu from the steamer. Be careful—the steam can burn your hands and the tofu is quite fragile. Transfer the tofu block to a cutting board and cut it into 1-inch cubes. Set aside along with the steamed mushrooms.

6. In a small bowl or teacup, whisk the arrowroot and water until well combined. Whisk this into the saucepan with the simmering soy sauce mixture, just until thickened; stir in the cubed tofu, the steamed mushrooms, and the rice vinegar. Cover the pan, remove from the heat, and let stand for 10 minutes before serving.

> **N O T E :** Red cooked tofu is traditionally made with dark soy sauce, an aged condiment available in most Asian markets and in the Asian section of some gourmet stores. You can also use regular soy sauce, or even low-sodium soy sauce. In any event, do not use the confusingly named "light soy sauce," a very pungent, ketchup-like sauce.

VEGGIE BURGERS 💼

makes **2 large patties**

Similar to falafel, these burgers are made with chopped vegetables, but are bound together with rolled oats rather than chickpeas. Allow the burgers to rest for at least an hour before frying so that the oats become sticky enough to hold the vegetables in place. Serve the patties on hamburger buns with tomato, lettuce, ketchup, or mustard; in pita rounds, with shredded lettuce and a creamy salad dressing; or simply on their own, with chutney and mustard on the side.

1 tablespoon plus 2 teaspoons olive oil

2 medium scallions, thinly sliced

½ cup plus 1 tablespoon rolled oats (do not use quick cooking)

1 small zucchini (about 4 ounces), thinly sliced

1 small carrot, shredded

1½ tablespoons tahini (see page 54)

1 tablespoon chopped fresh parsley, or 1 teaspoon dried parsley

1 teaspoon soy sauce

½ teaspoon Dijon mustard

¼ teaspoon freshly ground black pepper

¼ cup flour, plus more for your hands

1. Heat a small skillet over medium heat. Swirl in 2 teaspoons of the oil, add the scallions, and cook for 2 minutes, just until soft. Scrape the scallions and any oil into a food processor fitted with the chopping blade or into a large blender. Add the oats, zucchini, carrot, tahini, parsley, soy sauce, mustard, and pepper. Process until smooth, scraping down the sides of the bowl as necessary. Transfer the mixture to a medium bowl; cover and refrigerate for 1 hour. The recipe can be made in advance up to this point; store the covered mixture in the refrigerator for up to 2 days.

2. Place the flour on a large plate; dust your hands with flour as well. Form the vegetable mixture into two large, thin patties, 4 inches in diameter and about ½ inch thick. Dip them one at a time in the flour, coating both sides. Brush off any excess flour.

3. Heat a large skillet over medium heat. Swirl in the remaining 1 tablespoon oil, then slip the patties into the pan and cook for 3 minutes. Turn, using a wide spatula because the patties are fragile, and cook for about 3 more minutes, or until lightly browned. Serve at once.

CRISPY POLENTA WITH MUSHROOMS

makes **2 servings**

Polenta, a northern Italian classic, is nothing more than a thickened cornmeal mixture. But when fried crisp in olive oil and topped with sautéed mushrooms, it's definitely a meal for two, warm and satisfying. Serve this entrée with a light fruit salad, dressed with lemon juice, chopped rosemary, and olive oil.

1½ teaspoons unsalted butter, at room temperature, plus additional for buttering the pan
1½ cups water
½ cup coarse yellow cornmeal
2 tablespoons freshly grated Parmigiano-Reggiano (about ½ ounce)
½ teaspoon salt
2 tablespoons olive oil
1 small onion, thinly sliced
8 ounces cremini or white button mushrooms, cleaned and thinly sliced (see Note)

6 tablespoons dry vermouth
1 tablespoon tomato paste
½ teaspoon chopped fresh thyme, or ¼ teaspoon dried thyme
½ teaspoon chopped fresh rosemary, or ¼ teaspoon chopped dried rosemary
¼ teaspoon freshly ground black pepper

1. Butter a 1-quart round soufflé dish; set aside.

2. Bring the water to a boil in a medium saucepan set over high heat. Stir in 1 tablespoon of the cornmeal with a wooden spoon, then immediately reduce the heat to low. Continue adding tablespoonfuls of the cornmeal, stirring each in before adding the next. Once all the cornmeal has been added, reduce the heat to very low and continue cooking for about 15 minutes, stirring constantly, until the polenta begins to leave a film on the bottom and sides of the saucepan. In these small quantities, polenta can scorch, so keep the flame low and stir constantly.

3. Stir in the 1½ teaspoons butter, the cheese, and ¼ teaspoon of the salt. Pour the hot polenta mixture into the prepared casserole dish. Set aside to cool and firm up for at least 30 minutes while you prepare the mushrooms. You can also make the polenta up to a day in advance, storing it, covered, in the refrigerator; let it come back to room temperature before continuing with the recipe.

4. Heat a medium skillet or sauté pan over medium heat. Swirl in 1 tablespoon of the olive oil, then add the onion. Cook for 3 minutes, or until golden, stirring frequently. Add the mushrooms and continue cooking for about 5 minutes, or until they release their liquid and it is nearly evaporated, stirring occasionally.

5. Add the vermouth, tomato paste, thyme, and rosemary; bring the mixture to a simmer. Cover, reduce the heat to low, and simmer for 15 minutes, or until thickened like a sauce. Stir in the remaining ¼ teaspoon of salt and the pepper. Set aside off the heat, covered to keep warm.

6. Run a knife around the sides of the polenta to release it from the casserole dish. Turn the polenta out onto your work surface and cut it, like a pie, into six even wedges. Heat the remaining 1 tablespoon olive oil in a medium skillet or sauté pan set over medium heat. When the oil begins to smoke, carefully add the polenta wedges. Fry for about 4 minutes, or until lightly browned and crisp, turning once.

7. To serve, divide the wedges between two plates. Spoon the mushroom sauce around and over them. Serve immediately.

> **NOTE:** Any type of mushroom can work in this dish. For a decadent treat, use fresh porcini. Or mix fresh porcini with other mushrooms, such as shiitake, portobello, lobster, or hen of the wood, all cleaned and sliced into thin strips. Use a small, soft-bristle brush to remove any dirt.

"Pulled" Potato and Vegetable Sandwiches

makes 2 large or 4 small sandwiches

The idea for this vegetarian dish came from barbecue pulled pork sandwiches. In those, the meat is cooked until it can be pulled into threads. Here, the vegetables are shredded, then mixed into a vinegary barbecue sauce. If you like your sandwiches spicy, pass additional Tabasco sauce alongside. And pass various condiments as well, such as pickle relish, sliced tomatoes, and shredded lettuce.

⅔ cup ketchup

¼ cup plus 2 tablespoons cider vinegar

¼ cup plus 2 tablespoons water, plus more if necessary

2 tablespoons packed dark brown sugar

2 teaspoons dry mustard

2 teaspoons mild paprika

½ teaspoon celery seeds

½ teaspoon freshly ground black pepper

4 dashes Tabasco sauce, or to taste

1 medium carrot, shredded

1 small yellow-fleshed potato (about 4 ounces), such as Yukon Gold, peeled and shredded

1 very small Savoy cabbage (about 9 ounces), outer leaves removed, cored, and the remaining leaves shredded

½ teaspoon salt, or to taste

2 or 4 challah rolls, kaiser rolls, or hamburger buns (depending on if you want 2 large or 4 small sandwiches)

1. Stir the ketchup, vinegar, ¼ cup of the water, the brown sugar, dry mustard, paprika, celery seeds, pepper, and Tabasco sauce in a large saucepan set over medium heat until the sugar dissolves. Bring the mixture to a simmer, stir in the carrot and potato, and continue simmering for 5 minutes, stirring often.

2. Lay the cabbage on top of the simmering sauce and sprinkle the remaining 2 tablespoons of water over it. Do not stir. Cover the pan, reduce the heat to very low, and steam the cabbage for 3 minutes undisturbed.

3. Stir to thoroughly incorporate the cabbage, cover the pan, and continue cooking for 15 minutes, or until the vegetables are tender and the sauce is quite thick, stirring occasionally. If the mixture boils vigorously or starts to stick, reduce the heat even further, to the barest flame, then add water in 2 tablespoon increments, until the sauce is thick but not pastelike.

4. When the vegetables are tender, remove the pan from the heat, season with salt, and let stand, covered, for 5 minutes. Serve on challah rolls, kaiser rolls, or hamburger buns.

VEGETABLE TAGINE 💼

makes 2 generous servings

An aromatic Moroccan tagine is perhaps a cross between a stew and a casserole. It's usually served with a thin flatbread used to scoop up small portions of the dish. Tagine is also the name of the conical casserole dish in which the dish is traditionally made and served, but a 2½-quart covered casserole will hold the layered vegetables and spices just as well. Serve the tagine with plain couscous and Moroccan flatbread, or naan, an Indian flatbread.

1 teaspoon mild paprika
½ teaspoon ground cumin
½ teaspoon salt
¼ teaspoon ground cinnamon
¼ teaspoon freshly ground
  black pepper
2½ tablespoons water
1½ tablespoons almond oil or
  olive oil
1 teaspoon honey
1 small zucchini, thinly sliced
1 medium yellow-fleshed
  potato (about 6 ounces),
  such as Yukon Gold, thinly
  sliced
1 tablespoon chopped fresh
  parsley, or ¼ teaspoon
  dried parsley

4 dried, pitted dates, chopped
1 medium garlic clove, minced
1 large Italian plum tomato
  (about 4 ounces), thinly
  sliced
1 large carrot, thinly sliced
1 tablespoon chopped fresh
  cilantro, or ½ teaspoon
  dried cilantro
1 small onion, thinly sliced
  into rings
1 green Italian pepper
  (cubanel), cored, seeded,
  and cut into rings; or 1
  small green bell pepper,
  cored, seeded, and diced

1. Position the rack in the bottom third of the oven and preheat the oven to 350°F. Combine the paprika, cumin, salt, cinnamon, and pepper in a small bowl; set aside. Whisk the water, almond or olive oil, and honey in a second small bowl.

2. In a 2½-quart casserole or oven-safe pot, layer the following in this order: the sliced zucchini, ½ teaspoon of the spice mixture, the sliced

117

potato, ½ teaspoon of the spice mixture, the parsley, dates, garlic, the sliced tomato, ½ teaspoon of the spice mixture, the sliced carrot, ½ teaspoon of the spice mixture, the cilantro, onion, and pepper. Sprinkle any remaining spice mixture over the top, then pour the reserved honey mixture over the entire casserole.

3. Cover the casserole dish or pot with its lid or aluminum foil. Bake for 55 minutes, or until bubbly. Let stand for 5 minutes before serving.

SWISS CHARD ENCHILADAS

makes 4 enchiladas

These enchiladas are spiked with tequila, which gives them a delicate, slightly sour taste, a good foil to the sweet greens. Although the red, yellow, or white center "vein" in each leaf of Swiss chard must be cut away and discarded before the leaves are chopped, you needn't cut out the smaller, branching veins that run through the leaves. If you wish, you can chop the larger stems, freeze them, then later toss them into long-simmered soups and stews. Dried New Mexican chiles are available in most gourmet markets, all Mexican markets, and from outlets listed in the Source Guide (page 269).

FOR THE SAUCE

1 tablespoon canola or other vegetable oil
2 large shallots, chopped
1 large garlic clove, minced
One 14½-ounce can vegetable stock (regular, low-fat, or nonfat, but preferably low-sodium)
¼ cup tequila (see Note)
6 dried red New Mexican chiles, stemmed and seeded
1 tablespoon chopped fresh oregano, or 2 teaspoons dried oregano
½ teaspoon salt

FOR THE ENCHILADAS

2 tablespoons pine nuts
2 tablespoons canola or other vegetable oil, plus additional for the baking dish
2 medium garlic cloves, minced
1 small bunch red or yellow Swiss chard (about 12 ounces), stems and center veins removed, leaves roughly chopped
2 teaspoons chopped fresh oregano, or 1 teaspoon dried oregano
½ teaspoon ground cinnamon
½ teaspoon salt
¼ cup water
Four 10- to 12-inch flour tortillas
¾ cup shredded aged white Cheddar or Monterey Jack (about 3 ounces)

1. To make the sauce, heat a medium skillet over medium-high heat. Swirl in the oil, then add the shallots. Cook for 2 minutes, or until soft and fragrant, stirring frequently. Add the garlic, cook for 20 seconds, then stir in the stock and tequila. The tequila may ignite—if so, cover the pan and remove it from the heat for 30 seconds.

2. Stir in the chiles, oregano, and salt. Bring the mixture to a simmer, cover, reduce the heat to low, and simmer for 20 minutes, until the chiles are soft, stirring once or twice.

3. Transfer the chile mixture to a food processor fitted with the chopping blade or a large blender. Pulse twice to chop the chiles, then process until smooth, scraping down the sides of the bowl as necessary. Set aside. (The dish can be made up to this point in advance; let the sauce cool completely, then store it, covered, in the refrigerator for up to 2 days.)

4. To make the enchiladas, heat a large skillet over medium heat. Add the pine nuts and toast for about 3 minutes, or until lightly browned and fragrant, stirring frequently. Remove the pine nuts from the skillet and set them aside.

5. Return the skillet to medium heat, swirl in the oil, then add the garlic and cook for 30 seconds, just until lightly browned. Add the chopped Swiss chard, oregano, cinnamon, and salt. Toss with tongs or two large wooden spoons until thoroughly combined, then pour in the water. Cover the skillet, reduce the heat to low, and steam the chard for 10 minutes.

6. Uncover the skillet, toss the mixture thoroughly, then raise the heat to high and boil for about 1 minute, or until any excess liquid is evaporated. Transfer the filling to a bowl and set aside to cool slightly.

7. Position the rack in the bottom third of the oven and preheat the oven to 350°F. Oil an 8-inch square baking dish. Lay one tortilla on a clean, dry work surface. Spoon one-quarter of the sautéed chard mixture down the center of the tortilla. Top with 1½ tablespoons shredded cheese and ½ tablespoon toasted pine nuts. Roll the tortilla closed and place seam down in the prepared baking dish. Repeat with the remaining three tortillas.

8. Pour the prepared sauce over the rolled tortillas in the dish, covering them completely. Sprinkle with the remaining cheese and bake uncovered for 30 minutes, or until bubbly. Let stand for 5 minutes before serving.

> NOTE: Use the best tequila you can comfortably afford. High-quality tequila is made entirely from the root and heart of the blue agave plant (often labeled "100% blue agave" on the bottle). It is available in a clear variety, bottled right after distillation, as well as "reposado" (rested in oak for up to two years) or "anejo" (aged in oak for up to twenty years).

Fish

There's only one rule when it comes to cooking fish: however you cook it, don't cook it too long. So nothing beats fish for a quick, healthy dinner. What's more, fish is very forgiving: it takes to both simple and complex dishes with just a pinch of some pantry staples for good measure. So here is a set of simple stir-fries and sautés, a few hearty baked dishes, and a couple of ideas fit for more leisurely meals, all served up for two.

SHRIMP WITH PEPPERS AND GARLIC ⏱

makes **2 servings**

This quick shrimp sauté is served up with quite a bit of garlic. For best results, add the oil and the garlic to the skillet at the same time, so the garlic is coated in the oil before it starts to cook, then watch it carefully so that it doesn't brown, blacken, or burn—the point is simply to infuse the oil with garlic. Red bell peppers, albeit more costly, are slightly sweeter than the common green ones, and so balance the flavors better; but feel free to substitute any color bell pepper. Serve this sauté hot from the pan, over rice, cooked noodles, or wilted greens.

⅔ pound medium shrimp (about 20 shrimp at 30 per pound), peeled and deveined

2 teaspoons all-purpose flour

½ teaspoon salt

¼ teaspoon freshly ground black pepper

3 tablespoons olive oil

3 or 4 large garlic cloves, thinly sliced

3 medium scallions, cut into 1-inch pieces

1 red bell pepper, stemmed, cored, and thinly sliced

¼ cup dry vermouth or white wine

1. Place the shrimp in a medium bowl and sprinkle with the flour, salt, and pepper. Toss gently to coat, then set aside.

2. Heat a medium skillet or sauté pan over very low heat. Add the oil and garlic all at once; cook and stir for about 3 minutes, or until the garlic becomes very aromatic. Raise the heat to medium, add the scallions and pepper, and cook for 2 more minutes, just until the scallions wilt, stirring constantly.

3. Pour the coated shrimp into the pan and cook for about 3 minutes, or until the shrimp are firm and pink, stirring occasionally. Raise the heat to high, pour the vermouth into the pan, and bring the mixture to a boil. Boil for just 20 seconds, stirring constantly, until the sauce is thickened and reduced. Serve immediately.

Other Oils

Change the taste of this dish by changing the oil used to sauté the garlic. For a deeper, spicier taste, substitute an equivalent amount of mustard seed oil. For a brighter taste, use grapeseed oil. Or use an infused oil, like basil oil or sundried tomato oil.

ORANGE SCALLOP STIR-FRY

makes 2 **servings**

This stir-fry is a light, fresh take on that Chinese take-out favorite, orange beef. As with any stir-fry, the cooking goes quickly, so have all the ingredients prepared before you begin. Serve over rice, or for a more authentic taste, over steamed mustard greens or spinach.

1 large orange	2 teaspoons water
2 tablespoons black Chinese vinegar, or 1½ tablespoons balsamic vinegar	2 tablespoons peanut oil
	4 dried Chinese red chiles, or ¼ teaspoon red pepper flakes
1 tablespoon soy sauce	
1 tablespoon Shao Shing (see page 13)	2 large garlic cloves, slivered
	⅔ pound sea scallops
1 teaspoon sugar	½ pound pencil-thin asparagus spears, cut into 1-inch sections (see Note)
1 teaspoon arrowroot or cornstarch	

1. Use a vegetable peeler to peel wide strips of the zest from the orange. You should have about 8 strips when done, each about 2 inches long; set them aside. Cut the orange in half and squeeze 2 tablespoons juice into a small bowl. Whisk the vinegar, soy sauce, Shao Shing, and sugar into the orange juice; set aside. Whisk the arrowroot or cornstarch and water in a second small bowl or a teacup until smooth; set this aside as well.

2. Heat a wok or medium saucepan over very low heat. Add the oil, chiles, garlic, and orange zest all at once, then stir-fry for about 3 minutes to infuse the oil, until the mixture is very aromatic. Raise the heat to medium-high, add the scallops, and stir-fry for 2 minutes, or until firm and opaque. Add the asparagus and sauté for just 30 seconds.

3. Pour in the prepared vinegar mixture and cook for about 15 seconds, stirring constantly, until the sauce comes to a simmer and coats the seafood and vegetables. Quickly rewhisk the arrowroot mixture to reincorporate any solids, push the scallops and vegetables to the side of the pan, and pour this mixture into the simmering sauce. Stir well and cook for about 20 seconds, or until the sauce thickens. Serve immediately.

> N O T E : If the asparagus spears are thicker than a standard #2 pencil, peel them using a vegetable peeler to that size, then slice them into 1-inch sections.

Other Orange Stir-Fries
Substitute ²/₃ pound medium shrimp (about 20 shrimp at 30 per pound), peeled and deveined, for the scallops.

Or substitute ²/₃ pound chicken tenders, cut into 1-inch sections, for the scallops. Stir-fry them an extra minute in the flavored oil to make sure they're cooked through.

Or omit the shellfish entirely and stir in 2 cups beet greens, cleaned and stemmed, in place of the scallops.

STEAMED MUSSELS THREE WAYS ⏱

makes **2 servings**

Thanks to mollusk farms on both coasts, mussels are now widely available and quite fresh. The trick is not to overcook them, so serve them the moment they've steamed open.

MUSSELS STEAMED IN COCONUT CURRY

Indian flavors infuse the coconut milk in this dish, best served with naan, an Indian flatbread, flour tortillas, or a crunchy baguette—so you can soak up every drop of the sauce. Red Thai curry paste is an oil-free, concentrated paste, hotter than yellow Thai curry paste because of the additional cayenne pepper. It's available in Indian markets and the Asian aisle of some supermarkets. Take care not to confuse it with Chinese red chili paste.

1½ tablespoons canola or other vegetable oil
3 small scallions, thinly sliced
1 small green bell pepper, seeded, cored, and chopped
2 medium garlic cloves, minced
2 tablespoons peeled, minced fresh ginger
1 tablespoon mango chutney
1 tablespoon red Thai curry paste, or 1 tablespoon yellow Thai curry paste

½ teaspoon salt
One 14-ounce can coconut milk (regular or low-fat)
2 pounds mussels, scrubbed and debearded
¼ cup chopped fresh cilantro, or 1½ tablespoons dried cilantro

1. Heat a large saucepan over medium-high heat. Swirl in the oil, then add the scallions and bell pepper. Cook for 1 minute, or until wilted and lightly browned, stirring constantly. Add the garlic and cook for just 10 seconds, stirring constantly. Then stir in the ginger, mango chutney, Thai curry paste, and salt; cook for about 10 more seconds, or just until the chutney melts and the paste dissolves, stirring constantly. Pour in the coconut milk and bring the mixture to a boil.

2. Dump in the mussels, stir thoroughly, then cover the pan and reduce the heat to medium-low. Simmer for about 5 minutes, or until the mussels open. Remove from the heat and stir in the cilantro. Cover and let stand for 5 minutes off the heat to infuse the flavors before serving.

STEAMED MUSSELS JAPANESE-STYLE

makes 2 light servings

Of the three mussel dishes presented here, this one has the brightest, cleanest taste. To ensure that it stays that way, choose a good brand of sake, preferably a filtered sake. Pickled ginger is available in Asian markets and in the Asian section of almost all supermarkets; look for pale pink slices that have not discolored to brown. Wasabi paste, made from a pungent, horseradish-like root, is now available in squeeze tubes. Once opened, it can be stored in the refrigerator for up to a year.

¾ cup sake	2 teaspoons wasabi paste
½ cup sushi-style pickled ginger, chopped	2 pounds mussels, scrubbed and debearded
3 tablespoons soy sauce	

1. Whisk the sake, ginger, soy sauce, and wasabi paste in a large saucepan set over medium-high heat until the wasabi dissolves. Bring the mixture to a boil.

2. Add the mussels, stir well, then cover the pan and reduce the heat to medium. Cook for about 5 minutes, or until the mussels open, stirring once or twice. Serve immediately.

MUSSELS STEAMED IN
BRANDY WITH APPLES AND SAGE

makes 2 **servings**

Here's a New England take on mussels, perfect for a fall evening.
Serve this dish with a crisp, chilled Sauvignon Blanc or a California
Chardonnay.

2 tablespoons unsalted butter,
at room temperature
1 small onion, thinly sliced
2 celery ribs, thinly sliced
1 large tart apple, such as
Granny Smith or McIntosh,
peeled, cored, halved, and
thinly sliced
2 teaspoons chopped fresh
sage, or 1 teaspoon rubbed
sage

¼ teaspoon grated nutmeg
¼ teaspoon salt
¼ teaspoon freshly ground
black pepper
One 8-ounce bottle clam juice,
or ½ cup water
¼ cup brandy
2 pounds mussels, scrubbed
and debearded

1. Melt the butter in a large saucepan set over medium heat. Add the
onion and cook for about 3 minutes, until golden, stirring constantly.
Add the celery and apple; cook for about 2 more minutes, or just until
the apple softens. Then stir in the sage, nutmeg, salt, and pepper and
cook for just 10 seconds, or until the spices are redolent.

2. Raise the heat to high and pour in the clam juice and the brandy. (If
the mixture in the pan ignites because of the brandy, cover the
saucepan and take it off the heat for 30 seconds, or until the flame goes
out.) Cook for about 2 minutes, or until the liquid reduces by half. Stir
in the mussels and bring the mixture back to a simmer. Cover the pan,
reduce the heat to medium-low, and cook for 5 minutes, or just until
the mussels open. Serve at once.

On Mussels

Buy mussels "loose"—that is, not in prepackaged bags—so you can inspect them. They should smell fresh and briny, never fishy or oily; they should all be closed.

When you get them home, store them for no more than 12 hours in your refrigerator in a large bowl loosely covered with damp paper towels.

When you're ready to use them, rinse them in cool water, scrubbing the shells lightly with a potato brush or your fingernails to get rid of any sand. Discard any mussels that are open and will not close when tapped or gently squeezed. Then debeard them—that is, remove the wiry hairs that sometimes protrude from the shells; pull these off just before you cook the mussels because removing the beards fatally damages the mollusks.

Once cooked, always err on the side of safety: discard any that do not open.

CRAWFISH STUFFED ARTICHOKES 🍷🍷

makes **2 stuffed artichokes**

Here's a dish for a small celebration: an anniversary or a promotion. The artichokes are stuffed with a cheese-laced, spicy crawfish stuffing. For a larger meal, start off with Escarole, White Bean, and Roasted Garlic Soup (page 22); for dessert, serve Chocolate Chip Espresso Cookies (page 208). Because artichokes turn brown when cut, work quickly with the lemon juice to cover any cut areas; the acid in lemon juice will impede any discoloration. Look for cooked crawfish tail meat at most large supermarkets in the frozen seafood section, or buy it fresh at the fish counter of gourmet markets.

½ cup plain dried bread crumbs
1 small shallot, cut in quarters
1 small garlic clove, chopped
2 tablespoons freshly grated Parmigiano-Reggiano (about ½ ounce)
¼ cup chopped fresh parsley, or 1 tablespoon dried parsley
2 teaspoons chopped fresh oregano, or 1 teaspoon dried oregano

1 tablespoon chopped fresh basil, or 1 teaspoon dried basil
¼ teaspoon red pepper flakes
¼ teaspoon salt
4 tablespoons olive oil
8 ounces cooked crawfish tail meat (if frozen, thaw, rinse, drain, and squeeze dry)
2 large globe artichokes (about 12 ounces each)
1 large lemon, cut in half

1. To make the filling, place the bread crumbs, shallot, garlic, cheese, parsley, oregano, basil, red pepper flakes, and salt in a food processor fitted with the chopping blade or a large blender. Pulse four or five times, until well chopped. Add 2 tablespoons of the olive oil, then pulse to incorporate. Add the crawfish meat and pulse four or five times to chop and combine. The mixture should be coarsely chopped, not puréed or pastelike. Set aside. The recipe can be made in advance up to this point; store the filling, covered, in the refrigerator for up to 2 days. Let it come back to room temperature before proceeding.

2. Prepare the artichokes by first cutting off the stems so each artichoke has a flat bottom to stand on. Pull off any small, tough leaves (or petals, since artichokes are technically flowers) still adhering to the outside of the bottom, as well as the bottom two layers of larger leaves. Rub the bottoms of both artichokes with half of the lemon. Lay the artichokes on their sides on your work surface; use a heavy, serrated knife to cut off the top third of each. Rub the tops with the lemon half. Spread the leaves open and use a small spoon, preferably a grapefruit spoon, to scoop out the center, including the hairy fibers that come up off the choke. Rub the insides of each artichoke with the other half of the lemon.

3. Stuff about one-third of the crawfish mixture into the center of each artichoke. Use the remainder of the stuffing to fill in between the outer leaves, pressing down gently to pack the filling in. Stand the stuffed artichokes up in a 3-quart oval or round pot large enough so that they are not squeezed together. Add enough water to come up about ½ inch. Place the lemon halves in the pot, quartering them if necessary to fit. Drizzle the remaining 2 tablespoons of olive oil over and around the artichokes.

4. Set the pot over medium-high heat and bring the water to a boil. Cover, reduce the heat to low, and simmer for 40 minutes, or until the bottoms of the artichokes are tender when pierced with a knife.

5. Remove the artichokes from the pot, tent with foil to keep warm, and raise the heat to high. Boil any remaining liquid in the pot until it is reduced to about 2 tablespoons. Pour this reduced cooking liquid over the artichokes and serve immediately.

Not Just Crawfish

Substitute 15 medium precooked cocktail shrimp, cleaned and deveined, for the crawfish tail meat. Or substitute 8 ounces cooked lump crabmeat, picked over for shells and cartilage.

FISH FILLETS IN PARCHMENT

makes **2 servings**

Nothing is easier than baking fish in an envelope of parchment paper. Herbs and vegetables will melt into a sauce you can serve over the fillets or accompanying rice. Parchment paper—a thick paper safe for baking—is found with the aluminum foil and plastic wrap in supermarkets and gourmet stores. Jarred artichoke hearts and olives carry a lot of salt, so there's no salt added to the dish.

Two 18- to 20-inch-long pieces of parchment paper
Two ⅓-pound white-fleshed fish fillets, such as bass, snapper, orange roughy, tilapia, or cod, skinned and checked for bones
One 6-ounce jar marinated artichoke hearts, drained

8 cherry tomatoes
12 pitted black olives, preferably herbed Provençal olives
2 teaspoons olive oil
1 teaspoon lemon juice
¼ teaspoon freshly ground black pepper

1. Position the rack in the oven's center and preheat the oven to 450°F.

2. Lay one piece of parchment paper on top of the other on a large lipped baking sheet. Lay the fish fillets in the center of the paper. Top with the artichoke hearts, tomatoes, and olives. Drizzle with the olive oil and lemon juice; sprinkle with the pepper. Fold the parchment closed, crinkling it to make a tight seal.

3. Bake for 12 minutes, or until the fish is cooked through. Serve immediately by unwrapping the paper and placing one fillet on each of two plates. Top with the vegetables and any cooking liquid.

An Alternate Presentation
Wrap each fillet individually in parchment packets, topping each with half the spices and vegetables. Transfer one intact, baked packet to each of two plates; unwrap the packets and eat the fish and vegetables right out of them.

COD ROASTED OVER
SWISS CHARD AND GARLIC 💼

makes **2 servings**

In this quick dish, a cod fillet is set on a bed of steamed greens, then baked in the oven. It's light enough for a spring evening but comforting enough for a winter supper. If you like, substitute other light greens for the chard, such as beet greens, escarole, or dandelion greens.

¾ pound skinless cod fillet
3 tablespoons olive oil
½ teaspoon salt
¼ teaspoon freshly ground black pepper

1 pound Swiss chard, center stems removed, leaves shredded, washed but not dried
2 or 3 garlic cloves, slivered
2 teaspoons balsamic vinegar

1. Rub the cod fillet with 1 tablespoon of the olive oil; gently massage the salt and pepper into the flesh. Set aside.

2. Position the rack in the center of the oven and preheat the oven to 500°F. Heat a medium oven-safe skillet or sauté pan over low heat. Add the remaining 2 tablespoons olive oil and the garlic all at once, then cook for 2 minutes, taking care not to brown the garlic. Raise the heat to medium and lay the wet greens in the skillet. Toss them once or twice, to get the garlic strewn throughout the leaves, then cover the pan and steam the greens for about 3 minutes, or until they are wilted but not limp.

3. Uncover the pan and place the prepared cod fillet on top of the greens. Place the pan in the oven and roast the cod fillet and greens, uncovered, for about 10 minutes, until the cod is cooked through. To tell, either cut it open, or insert a thin dinner knife into the thickest part of the fillet, hold the knife in the flesh for 10 seconds, then remove it and touch its side to your lips, taking care not to cut yourself. The knife blade should feel warm (for a firmer fillet) or hot (for a fillet cooked through).

4. Remove the pan from the oven (be careful—it's quite hot), drizzle the balsamic vinegar over the cod fillet and greens while they're still in the pan, and serve immediately.

Cooking for Two

SNAPPER FILLETS SAUTÉED WITH ORANGE AND PECANS

makes **2 light servings**

Since the fillets are placed on top of salad greens, then dressed with a sauce from the pan, this easy, fresh-tasting sauté is something like a composed salad, ready in minutes. If you want a simpler dish, substitute a small 4-ounce can of orange sections, packed in water, drained and rinsed, along with 1 tablespoon orange juice for the fresh orange supremes. You can also substitute any number of thin fillets for the snapper, including talapia, orange roughy, or trout.

2 skinless snapper fillets (about 6 ounces each), checked over for bones	1 medium orange
	3 tablespoons olive oil
	1 small red onion, thinly sliced into rings
½ teaspoon salt	
½ teaspoon freshly ground black pepper	2 tablespoons pecan pieces
4 cups mixed salad greens, preferably baby greens (about 4 ounces)	1 teaspoon Champagne vinegar, or white wine vinegar

1. Season the fillets with ¼ teaspoon of the salt and ¼ teaspoon of the pepper; set them aside. Arrange half the greens on each of two dinner plates; set them aside as well.

2. Cut ¼ inch off the top and bottom of the orange, so that it will sit flat. Stand it on a cutting board, then cut down the sides of the fruit with a paring knife, following the fruit's natural curve, thereby removing the rind and the white pith underneath. You may also cut off a small amount of the flesh. Once the rind and pith are removed, hold the fruit in one hand over a small bowl and use a paring knife to cut between the membranes, letting the orange supremes and any juice fall into the bowl. Once all the supremes are removed, discard any remaining pith. You should have about ½ cup supremes and juice.

3. Heat a large skillet over medium heat. Swirl in 1 tablespoon of the oil, then slip the fish fillets into the pan. Cook for about 1 minute, then gently turn with a wide metal spatula and cook for about 2 more minutes. Once the fish is cooked through, transfer the fillets to the two prepared plates, placing them on top of the greens.

4. Add the remaining 2 tablespoons oil to the pan, then slide in the red onion rings and soften for about 1 minute, stirring often. Sprinkle in the pecans and sauté for 1 more minute, just until they begin to brown. Add the orange supremes and any juice, the vinegar, and the remaining salt and pepper. Cook for about 1 minute, or until the mixture is bubbling and slightly reduced, then pour as a dressing over each of the two plates, coating the fish and the greens. Serve immediately.

SOUTHWESTERN GLAZED SALMON

makes **2 servings**

Mayonnaise makes an easy but decadent glaze for salmon fillets—much like hollandaise sauce, but without the work. Here, it's spiked with lime and chili powder. Serve this easy entrée with a fresh salad of baby spinach leaves, walnuts, and soft goat cheese, dressed with a light vinaigrette.

Two 6-ounce salmon fillets
1 tablespoon olive oil
2 tablespoons chopped fresh cilantro, or 2 teaspoons dried cilantro
¼ cup mayonnaise (regular or low-fat, but not nonfat)

1½ teaspoons lime juice
1 small garlic clove, crushed
½ teaspoon chili powder
¼ teaspoon salt

1. Position the rack in the center of the oven and preheat the oven to 500°F. Rub the flesh and skin of the salmon fillets with the olive oil. (Doing this will also allow you to check for bones, so rub carefully but thoroughly. If you find any bones, pull them out with your fingers or a pair of tweezers.) Coat the flesh of the fillets with the chopped cilantro.

2. Mix the mayonnaise, lime juice, garlic, chili powder, and salt in a small bowl until uniform. Spoon this mixture on top of the fillets, spreading it out to cover the flesh.

3. Heat a large, oven-safe skillet, preferably cast-iron, over high heat. Add the fillets, skin side down. Shake once to make sure they don't stick; if they do, loosen gently with a spatula. Cook for just 1 minute, then place the skillet in the oven and bake for 5 minutes, or until the glaze is set and the salmon is cooked but still pink in the center. You can also check for doneness by inserting a knife into the flesh, then touching the side of the blade gently to your lips; it should feel warm. Serve at once.

SESAME TUNA STEAKS

makes 2 servings (with about ⅔ cup sauce)

Make sure you buy sushi-quality tuna, the freshest you can find. Look for ruby-red, almost translucent fillets or steaks without brown or white spots.

FOR THE SAUCE

6 tablespoons water

1½ tablespoons cornstarch

2 tablespoons rice vinegar (see page 12)

2 tablespoons sugar

1 tablespoon soy sauce

1 medium scallion, thinly sliced

1 teaspoon peeled, minced fresh ginger

¼ teaspoon red pepper flakes, or more to taste

1 tablespoon lime juice

FOR THE TUNA

¼ cup sesame seeds

1 teaspoon salt, preferably a coarse salt such as kosher salt

½ teaspoon freshly ground black pepper

Two 6-ounce sushi-grade tuna steaks, about 1 inch thick

3 tablespoons olive oil

1. To make the sauce, stir 1 tablespoon water with the cornstarch in a small bowl until pastelike; set aside. Mix the remaining 5 tablespoons water, the rice vinegar, sugar, soy sauce, scallion, ginger, red pepper flakes, and lime juice in a small saucepan set over high heat until the sugar dissolves. Bring to a boil, then whisk in the prepared cornstarch mixture in a slow, steady stream. Continue cooking and whisking about 10 seconds, or just until thickened. Remove the pan from the heat and whisk in the lime juice. Transfer the sauce to a serving bowl and cool to room temperature. The sauce can be made in advance; store it, covered, in the refrigerator for up to 3 days.

2. To prepare the fish, position the rack in the middle of the oven and preheat the oven to 450°F. Spread the sesame seeds on a dinner plate.

Coat each tuna steak with 1 tablespoon olive oil, massaging the oil into the fillet. Lay one steak on the plate; press down to coat with the sesame seeds. Turn, press again, then roll the sides in the sesame seeds. Set aside and repeat with the other tuna steak. Season both with salt and pepper.

3. Heat a large, oven-safe skillet, preferably cast-iron, over medium-high heat. Swirl in the remaining 1 tablespoon of olive oil, then gently lay the tuna steaks in the pan. Cook for just 30 seconds. Turn with a wide spatula, taking care not to scrape off the sesame seed coating. Cook for an additional 30 seconds, then place the pan in the oven and bake for 3 minutes for rare (red and warm inside), 4 for medium-rare (pink and hot), or 6 for medium (cooked through). Besides cutting the steaks open to check, you can also insert a dinner knife into the thickest part of the flesh, hold it there for 10 seconds, then gently touch the side of the knife to your lips. It should be slightly warm for rare, warm for medium-rare, and hot for medium.

4. Transfer the steaks to two serving plates with a spatula. Let stand for 3 minutes at room temperature. To serve, drizzle the prepared sauce over each steak.

Spicing It Up
You can add any number of spices to the sesame seed mixture before coating the fish, including any one of the following:

> 1 tablespoon unsweetened coconut, ground to a powder in a spice mill or coffee grinder
> 1 teaspoon curry powder
> 1 teaspoon dried oregano
> ½ teaspoon ground cinnamon
> ½ teaspoon red pepper flakes
> ¼ teaspoon cayenne pepper

STEAMED WHOLE SNAPPER WITH PIMIENTO SAUCE 🧳

makes 1 whole steamed fish, or 2 servings

To make this impressive entrée, you steam the whole fish on a bed of parsley set on a dinner plate or small platter. A fish steamer will make it in a snap, but a small roasting pan with a tight-fitting lid will do just as well. So that the plate doesn't rest in the water, set it up on four "columns" made from thick potato slices, which you will discard when done. When buying a whole snapper, look for clear, bright eyes, the true measure of a fish's freshness. The sauce, by the way, is good on its own, as a dip for bread and celery, or as a light glaze for barbecued chicken.

1 teaspoon sesame seeds
One 6-ounce jar pimientos, drained
1 small garlic clove, cut in half
4 teaspoons sesame oil
2 teaspoons rice vinegar (see page 12)
¾ teaspoon salt
2 dashes Tabasco sauce, or to taste

1½ to 2 pounds whole snapper, cleaned and gutted
½ teaspoon freshly ground black pepper
3 large scallions, cut in half
1 small bunch flat-leaf parsley
1 medium baking potato

1. Toast the sesame seeds by placing them in a small, dry skillet set over medium-low heat for about 3 minutes, tossing occasionally. They should be quite fragrant—a paler brown color will indicate a lighter taste; deeper brown, a nuttier flavor. Set aside.

2. Place the pimientos, garlic, 2 teaspoons of the sesame oil, the rice vinegar, ¼ teaspoon of the salt, and the Tabasco sauce in a food processor fitted with the chopping blade, in a mini food processor, or in a large blender. Process until smooth, scraping down the sides of the bowl as necessary. Set aside.

3. Rinse the fish with cold water, then pat it dry with paper towels. Score the skin twice on each side with a sharp knife, just deep enough to cut through the skin but not so deep as to cut through the flesh to the bones. Rub the fish on both sides with the remaining 2 teaspoons of sesame oil, the remaining ½ teaspoon of salt, and the pepper. Stuff the belly with the scallions.

4. Place an inch of water in a roasting pan or fish steamer with a tight-fitting lid. (You can also use aluminum foil as a cover.) Set the pan over high heat and bring the water to a boil. Meanwhile, place the parsley on a dinner plate or an oval platter that fits in the steamer or roasting pan; nestle the fish on top of the parsley. A piece of the tail and some of the head may hang off the sides of the plate.

5. Cut the ends off the potato, then cut it into four equal pieces, like stout columns. These four pieces will become the base for the plate holding the fish in the steamer or roasting pan. Place these potato sections in the simmering water, then set the plate with the fish on top of them. Cover the pan and steam for 15 minutes, or just until the flesh flakes when gently pulled with a fork.

6. Transfer the fish and parsley from the steaming plate to a clean serving platter using two large spatulas. Pour the pimiento-sesame sauce around the fish, then sprinkle the entire platter with the toasted sesame seeds. Serve immediately.

SMOKED TROUT CREAM CHEESE FRITTATA WITH DILL SAUCE

makes **2 servings**

Here's a quick meal for two—whether for breakfast, lunch, or dinner. Unlike an omelet, a frittata doesn't require any fancy flipping; instead, the skillet is covered and the egg mixture is allowed to cook on the stovetop. Look for firm smoked trout fillets that are light beige, not browned, a result of overheating during smoking.

2 tablespoons unsalted butter
1 small onion, chopped
6 large eggs, at room
   temperature
2 tablespoons milk (regular,
   low-fat, or nonfat)
¼ teaspoon freshly ground
   black pepper

4 ounces smoked trout,
   skinned and roughly
   chopped
2 ounces cream cheese
   (regular, low-fat, or
   nonfat), cut into ¼-inch
   pieces
Dill Sauce (recipe follows)

1. Melt the butter in an ovenproof 10-inch skillet, preferably cast-iron or nonstick, over low heat. Stir in the onion and cook for about 6 minutes, or until soft and golden, stirring occasionally. Meanwhile, whisk the eggs, milk, and pepper in a medium bowl.

2. Once the onion is golden, pour the egg mixture into the skillet. Gently pull back the edges of the egg mixture with a heat-safe rubber spatula or a wooden spoon, allowing more raw egg to come into contact with the hot skillet. Sprinkle the top with the smoked trout and cream cheese. Cover and cook for 10 minutes, or just until the frittata is set. Meanwhile, preheat the broiler.

3. When the frittata is set, place the skillet 4 to 6 inches below the broiler. Cook for 30 seconds, just until the top is lightly browned. Loosen the frittata from the pan with a heat-safe rubber spatula or any spatula safe for a nonstick pan. Slip it onto a serving platter. To serve, drizzle the dill sauce over the frittata, or serve it on the side.

DILL SAUCE

1½ tablespoons rice vinegar
(see page 12)
1 teaspoon Dijon mustard
2 teaspoons chopped fresh dill,
or 1 teaspoon dried dill
¼ teaspoon sugar

¼ teaspoon freshly ground
black pepper
¼ cup olive oil, preferably
extra-virgin olive oil

Whisk the vinegar and mustard in a small bowl until uniform. Stir in the dill, sugar, and pepper, then add the olive oil by drizzling it into the mixture in a thin stream while whisking constantly; continue whisking until the sauce is emulsified.

Chicken, Turkey, *and* Duck

More often than not, when you're cooking for two, chicken's what's for dinner. So here are some small dishes that are big on flavor and convenience—some easy sautés, a couple of stir-fries, even a recipe for quick and delicious duck breasts. You'll also find two of the classics—baked chicken and turkey with dressing—reinvented so you can enjoy them when you're cooking in small batches.

SAUTÉED
CHICKEN WITH RADISHES ⏱

makes **2 servings**

For too long, radishes have been relegated to the relish tray. Cooked, they turn sweet with a little spicy kick. For this simple sauté, look for whole, bright red radishes, preferably ones still attached to their greens—an assurance that they've been recently picked, rather than stored in a warehouse. Serve this dish with mashed potatoes and steamed green beans with slivered almonds, or steamed broccoli with pine nuts, or wash the radish greens, toss them with ½ teaspoon sugar and ½ teaspoon salt, and steam briefly for an interesting side dish.

Two 6-ounce boneless, skinless
chicken breast halves
½ teaspoon salt, or to taste
¼ teaspoon freshly ground
black pepper
1½ tablespoons olive oil
4 large radishes, washed for
sand and thinly sliced

¼ cup dry vermouth
2 teaspoons Champagne
vinegar, or white wine
vinegar
1 tablespoon unsalted butter,
at room temperature

1. Place a sheet of plastic wrap on your work surface, lay the two chicken breasts on top with about 4 inches between them, and cover with a second sheet of plastic wrap. Pound the breasts to a ¼-inch thickness, using the smooth side of a meat mallet or the bottom of a heavy saucepan. Remove from the plastic wrap, season the breasts with salt and pepper, and set aside.

2. Heat a large skillet or sauté pan over medium heat. Swirl in the oil, then slip the seasoned breasts into the pan. Sauté for 3 minutes, then turn and sauté for 3 more minutes, or until lightly browned and cooked through. Transfer to two dinner plates with tongs or a slotted spoon, tent the plates loosely with foil to keep the breasts warm, and return the pan to medium heat without removing any of the pan's residual fat.

3. Stir in the sliced radishes and sauté for about 2 minutes, or until they begin to go limp and are very fragrant. Pour in the vermouth and scrape up any browned bits on the bottom of the pan. Bring the vermouth to a simmer, cook for about 15 seconds, just until slightly reduced, then pour in the vinegar. Stir once or twice, then swirl in the butter and take the pan off the heat. Keep stirring until the butter is melted and incorporated into the sauce. Remove the foil from the breasts and pour this sauce evenly over each of them, spooning radishes onto the plates as well. Serve at once.

LEMON CHICKEN SAUTÉ

makes **2 servings**

Nothing complicated or unusual here—just a satisfying dinner in no time. Buy the best black olives you can find, preferably the small ones from Nyons or other varieties from Provence. Serve this meal with rice or roasted new potatoes, and finish it off with strawberry sorbet.

3 tablespoons all-purpose flour
½ teaspoon salt
½ teaspoon freshly ground
  black pepper
Two 6-ounce boneless, skinless
  chicken breast halves,
  pounded thin (see step 1 of
  Sautéed Chicken with
  Radishes, page 148)
1 tablespoon unsalted butter,
  at room temperature
  (see Note)

1 tablespoon olive oil
1½ tablespoons chopped pitted
  black olives
½ teaspoon grated lemon zest
¼ cup dry vermouth
3 tablespoons lemon juice
  (juice from 1 medium
  lemon)

1. Mix the flour, salt, and pepper together on a large dinner plate. Dredge the breasts in the flour mixture, coating both sides. Knock off any excess flour, then set them aside.

2. Melt the butter with the oil in a large skillet or sauté pan set over medium heat. Add the prepared chicken breasts and cook for 3 minutes. Turn and cook for about 3 more minutes, until browned and cooked through. Transfer the breasts to two dinner plates, tent them with foil to keep warm, and return the pan to medium heat without removing any of the pan's residual fat.

3. Stir in the olives and lemon zest and cook for about 20 seconds, just until sizzling. Pour in the vermouth and lemon juice, raise the heat to high, and bring the mixture to a simmer. Boil for 1 minute, or until slightly reduced, scraping up any browned bits on the bottom of the pan. Remove the foil from the breasts and pour this sauce evenly over them, dotting them with black olives. Serve immediately.

NOTE: You can use 2 tablespoons olive oil, rather than a mixture of butter and olive oil. Or you can use 2 tablespoons unsalted butter, provided you lower the heat so that the butter doesn't burn. The chicken breasts may then take a minute or two longer to cook through. Once you add the vermouth, raise the heat to high as indicated.

BAKED CHICKEN WITH SQUASH AND CHARD 🧳

makes **2 servings**

With a whole, bone-in chicken breast (two breasts still attached by the center bone), you can make a baked chicken dinner for two any night of the week. Here, the whole breast is set over a bed of greens and squash, but there are endless variations.

3 tablespoons unsalted butter, at room temperature

1 tablespoon minced fresh sage, or 1 teaspoon rubbed sage

¼ teaspoon salt

¼ teaspoon freshly ground black pepper

1 whole bone-in chicken breast (1½ to 1¾ pounds), ribs removed

1 small onion, minced

1 small delicata or kabocha squash (about ¾ pound),

peeled, seeded, and cut into ½-inch cubes, or 1 cup peeled and seeded butternut squash, cut into ½-inch cubes

1 small bunch red or yellow Swiss chard (about 8 ounces), stalks and thick veins removed, the leaves roughly chopped

¼ cup dry vermouth

2 tablespoons maple syrup

¼ teaspoon ground cinnamon

1. Position the rack in the center of the oven and preheat the oven to 375°F. Mix 1 tablespoon of the butter, 1 teaspoon of the fresh sage or ½ teaspoon of the rubbed sage, the salt, and pepper in a small bowl until smooth and pastelike. Rub this mixture over the chicken breast, particularly coating the skin and any exposed meat. If you wish, gently pull the skin up by starting at the thin end of the breast and slipping your finger between the skin and the meat; massage some of this paste directly onto the meat under the skin before pressing the skin back down onto the meat. Set aside.

2. Melt the remaining 2 tablespoons of butter in a large skillet or sauté pan set over medium heat. Stir in the onion and cook for 3 minutes, or until golden, stirring occasionally. Scoop in the cubed squash and cook for about 4 minutes, or until slightly softened, stirring often. Add the chard. There will be quite a lot of greens, so use tongs or two wooden spoons to gently turn the mixture until the onions and squash are evenly distributed throughout the chard leaves. Pour the vermouth over the greens, cover, and cook for about 2 minutes, or until the chard wilts.

3. Stir in the maple syrup, the remaining sage, and the cinnamon. Cook, uncovered, for about 4 minutes, or until the liquid in the pan has reduced to a glaze, stirring frequently.

4. Mound this vegetable mixture on a 10-inch pie plate. Nestle the prepared chicken breast into the vegetables, mounding them up into the hollow of the ribs. Bake for 45 minutes, or until the chicken is browned and cooked through, or until an instant-read thermometer inserted into the thickest part of the flesh registers 160°F. Remove from the oven, tent with foil, and let stand at room temperature for 5 minutes. To serve, either carve the breast as you would a whole roast chicken or split it in half down its center (i.e., along the breastbone) with poultry shears. Serve with the roasted vegetable mixture on the side.

Variations

Replace the squash with equivalent amounts of yellow beets, turnips, or rutabagas. Replace the Swiss chard with mustard greens, spinach, or beet greens. You can also stir 1 tablespoon pine nuts, 1 tablespoon pecan pieces, or 1 tablespoon sliced blanched almonds into the vegetable mixture before mounding it in the pie plate and baking it.

STUFFED CHICKEN BREASTS

makes **2 stuffed breasts**

In this dish, boneless, skinless chicken breasts are stuffed with thin slices of prosciutto, provolone, and arugula, and the accompanying Marsala sauce is made right in the pan. Use only dry Marsala, a slightly bitter aperitif, not sweet Marsala, a dessert wine. This dish is best accompanied by mashed or roasted potatoes.

Two 6-ounce boneless, skinless chicken breast halves	⅛ teaspoon salt
4 paper-thin slices prosciutto (about 1 ounce)	⅛ teaspoon freshly ground black pepper
4 thin slices provolone (about 1½ ounces)	1 tablespoon olive oil
⅓ cup packed arugula, washed, stems removed	3 garlic cloves, minced
2 teaspoons balsamic vinegar	⅓ cup dry Marsala
	½ teaspoon tomato paste (see page 14)

1. Position the rack in the middle of the oven and preheat the oven to 250°F. Place a sheet of plastic wrap on your work surface, lay the chicken breasts on it about 4 inches apart, then cover with a second sheet. Pound the breasts to a ¼-inch thickness with the smooth side of a meat mallet or the bottom of a heavy saucepan. Remove the top piece of plastic wrap. Lay two slices of prosciutto on top of each flattened breast, folding the prosciutto back from the breasts' sides so that there's a ¼-inch border of uncovered chicken all around the breasts.

2. Think of each breast as divided in half. Cover one half of each breast with two slices of provolone, then lay half the arugula over each breasts' provolone slices. Sprinkle ½ teaspoon of balsamic vinegar over each pile of arugula. Using the bottom sheet of plastic wrap as a guide, fold the non-cheese-and-arugula half of the breast up and over the cheese-and-arugula half. Press the breasts' edges closed to seal them, thus encasing the filling. Season the outside of the breasts with salt and pepper.

3. Heat a large skillet or sauté pan over medium heat. Swirl in the oil, then slip the stuffed breasts into the pan. Cook for about 6 minutes, or until browned; then turn and cook for about 6 more minutes. To keep the meat from sticking to the pan, shake the pan several times during the first minute of cooking to loosen the breasts. Transfer the cooked chicken breasts to an oven-safe plate and keep warm in the oven. Do not degrease the pan; return it to medium heat.

4. Add the garlic and cook for about 1 minute, or until sizzling, stirring often. Raise the heat to high and pour in the Marsala. Bring the wine to a boil, scraping up any bits on the bottom of the pan. Boil for 1 minute, then add the tomato paste and the remaining teaspoon of balsamic vinegar. Cook for about 15 seconds, just until the tomato paste melts into the sauce, stirring constantly. Return the breasts and any accumulated juices to the skillet. Heat through, about 1 minute per side. Transfer the breasts to two dinner plates and serve by pouring the sauce over the stuffed breasts.

SOUTHWESTERN
MOO SHU CHICKEN WRAPS

makes **2 tortilla wraps**

Here's a southwestern take on a Chinese stir-fry with Thai flavors. But it's not just innovation for its own sake—instead, there's a balance of flavors here, layered into a simple wrap. The chicken pieces and vegetables traditionally associated with moo shu dishes are quickly cooked in a wok, dressed with a Thai peanut sauce, then folded into flour tortillas. If you have peanut allergies, substitute cashew butter for the peanut butter and corn oil for the peanut oil.

2 tablespoons smooth peanut butter

1½ tablespoons soy sauce

1½ tablespoons water

2 teaspoons rice vinegar (see page 12)

1 teaspoon sugar

½ teaspoon chili powder

½ teaspoon freshly ground black pepper

2 tablespoons peanut oil

1 large boneless, skinless chicken breast half (about 8 ounces), sliced into thin strips

2 small scallions, thinly sliced

1 small garlic clove, minced

2 teaspoons peeled, minced fresh ginger

1 very small head green cabbage (about 8 ounces), cored, outer leaves removed, then the remaining leaves roughly chopped (about 2 cups; see Note)

1 cup fresh broccoli florets, or 1 cup frozen broccoli florets, thawed

1 medium portobello mushroom cap, finely chopped

Two 12- to 14-inch flour tortillas

1. Whisk the peanut butter, soy sauce, water, vinegar, sugar, chili powder, and pepper in small bowl until uniform; set aside.

2. Heat a wok or medium skillet over medium-high heat. Swirl in 1 tablespoon of the peanut oil, then add the chicken breast strips. Sauté for about 3 minutes, or until browned and cooked through, stirring frequently. Transfer the strips to a small plate and set aside.

3. Maintaining the heat under the wok or pan, swirl in the remaining 1 tablespoon of the peanut oil. Add the scallions, garlic, and ginger; stir-fry for 30 seconds, or until fragrant, tossing and stirring constantly. Then toss the cabbage, broccoli, and mushroom into the pan. Stir-fry for 1 minute, or just until the cabbage starts to go limp; then pour in the prepared peanut butter sauce. Cover the pan, reduce the heat to low, and cook for 4 minutes to wilt the cabbage and allow the mushrooms to release their liquid.

4. Uncover the pan, raise the heat to medium-high, and stir-fry for about 3 more minutes, or until any liquid in the pan is reduced to a glaze. Add the cooked chicken breast strips and any accumulated juices to the pan; stir-fry for about 1 minute, or until the chicken is heated through.

5. Lay the two tortillas on your work surface. Spoon half the mixture into the center of each. Roll into wraps and serve.

> N O T E : If you like, substitute 8 ounces baby bok choy, roughly chopped. Or use napa or savoy cabbage, although the heads are larger and will thus require you to use just half a head. Or substitute fresh baby spinach leaves for the cabbage.

CHICKEN AND DUMPLINGS
with PARSNIPS AND LEEKS 💼

makes **2 servings**

Here's a new, two-person version of the classic. The leeks melt into the stew, and the parsnips add just a touch of earthiness, more piquant than the traditional carrots, and so better able to cut through the creamy sauce. Slice them as thinly as possible to reduce the cooking time.

One 14½-ounce can chicken stock (regular, low-fat, or nonfat, but preferably low-sodium)

½ cup plus 2 teaspoons all-purpose flour

1 teaspoon baking powder

¾ teaspoon salt

½ teaspoon dry mustard

¼ teaspoon grated nutmeg

1 tablespoon solid vegetable shortening

3 tablespoons cold milk (regular, low-fat, or nonfat)

Two 6-ounce boneless, skinless chicken breast halves, each cut into four equal pieces

1 teaspoon mild paprika

¼ teaspoon freshly ground black pepper

1 tablespoon olive oil

1 medium parsnip, thinly sliced

1 leek, white part only, halved lengthwise, washed carefully of any sand, and thinly sliced

2 tablespoons chopped fresh parsley, or 2 teaspoons dried parsley

1 teaspoon fresh thyme, or ½ teaspoon dried thyme

1. To concentrate the flavors without having to simmer the sauce for hours, bring the stock to a boil in a small saucepan set over high heat. Continue boiling for about 3 minutes, or until reduced to 1¼ cups. Set aside.

2. Mix ½ cup of the flour, the baking powder, ¼ teaspoon of the salt, the dry mustard, and nutmeg in a medium bowl until uniform. Cut in the shortening with a pastry cutter or two forks until the mixture resembles coarse meal. Stir in the milk to make a dough. Make six dumpling balls about the size of Ping-Pong balls; cover with a dry towel and set aside. Season the chicken pieces with the paprika, pepper, and the remaining ½ teaspoon of salt; set aside as well.

3. Heat a large skillet over medium heat. Swirl in the oil, then add the parsnip and leek. Cook for 2 minutes, or until the leek is limp, stirring frequently. Sprinkle the remaining 2 teaspoons of flour evenly over the vegetables, cook for just 10 seconds, then stir well to incorporate. Add the chicken pieces and their juices to the skillet and cook for 2 minutes, turning once. Sprinkle in the parsley and thyme, then pour the reduced stock over the entire mixture. Bring it to a boil, stirring constantly and scraping up any browned bits on the bottom of the pan.

4. Lightly set the prepared dumplings on top of the simmering chicken mixture. Cover, reduce the heat to low, and cook for 15 minutes, until the chicken is cooked through and the dumplings are tender. If the stew starts to stick to the pan, reduce the heat even further. Once the chicken is cooked through, take the pan off the heat and let it stand, covered, for 5 minutes before serving.

OVEN-FRIED CHICKEN

makes 4 pieces of oven-fried chicken

Buttermilk gives this low-fat version of fried chicken the tang of the Southern classic. Panko are Japanese bread crumbs, excellent for any fried coating because they cook up exceedingly crisp. They're found in most Asian markets and gourmet stores, or in the Asian section of some supermarkets. If you can't find panko, use fresh bread crumbs made from two large slices of stale white bread, crusts removed. Purchased dried bread crumbs will burn in the oven.

¼ cup buttermilk (regular, low-fat, or nonfat)
1 cup panko (see headnote)
1 tablespoon canola or other vegetable oil
½ teaspoon mild paprika
¼ teaspoon salt
¼ teaspoon freshly ground black pepper
2 boneless, skinless chicken breast halves (about 8 ounces each)
2 chicken legs (about 6 ounces each), skin removed

1. Position the rack in the lower third of the oven and preheat the oven to 400°F. Pour the buttermilk into a large bowl, preferably a large, shallow soup bowl; set aside. Combine the panko, oil, paprika, salt, and pepper in a second large bowl.

2. Dip the chicken pieces first into the buttermilk, letting the excess drip back into the bowl, then into the panko mixture, coating all sides. Place the coated chicken pieces on a nonstick baking sheet, or a regular baking sheet lined with parchment paper, or a silicon baking sheet.

3. Bake for about 25 minutes, or until the chicken is cooked through but juicy. Serve at once.

CHICKEN TIKKA

makes **2 skewers**

One caveat before you make this easy Indian kabob: don't marinate the chicken for more than 2 hours because of bacterial growth associated with chicken and yogurt. For best results, use 8-inch metal skewers: they cook the chicken quickly by heating it from the inside while it broils on the outside. Serve this dish with jasmine rice and a salad of sliced cucumbers and radishes, dressed in lemon juice and olive oil with a pinch of sugar and salt.

⅓ cup plain yogurt
2 tablespoons mango chutney
1 teaspoon mild paprika
1 teaspoon salt
½ teaspoon dry mustard
½ teaspoon turmeric
½ teaspoon ground ginger
½ teaspoon freshly ground
   black pepper
⅛ teaspoon cayenne pepper

⅛ teaspoon ground cloves
Two 6-ounce boneless, skinless
   chicken breast halves,
   cut into 2-inch pieces
2 small white onions,
   quartered
1 lime, cut into quarters
2 metal skewers, at least
   8 inches long (see Note)

1. Whisk the yogurt, chutney, paprika, salt, mustard, turmeric, ginger, pepper, cayenne, and cloves in a medium bowl until smooth. Stir in the chicken pieces. Cover and refrigerate for at least 30 minutes but no more than 2 hours, tossing occasionally to coat the chicken thoroughly.

2. Preheat the broiler. Thread the chicken pieces onto the metal skewers—do not wipe off the marinade but discard the excess in the bowl. Place the chicken skewers on a broiler rack or a lipped baking sheet. Either can be lined with aluminum foil, if you wish, for an easier cleanup. Lay the onion quarters and lime wedges next to the skewers. Broil 4 to 6 inches from the heat source for about 12 minutes, or until the chicken is browned and cooked through, turning everything once.

Alternatively, you can grill the skewers for 12 minutes, turning once, on an oiled grill grate set over a grill preheated to medium heat or over medium-heat coals. In this case, skewer the lime wedges and onion quarters on a separate skewer before grilling. To serve, squeeze the broiled lime wedges over the chicken and onions.

NOTE: Metal skewers are available in most kitchenware stores and gourmet markets. If you use wood or bamboo skewers, soak them in water for 20 minutes before skewering the chicken to prevent scorching. You may then also need to increase the cooking time by 5 minutes.

LEMON GARLIC
CORNISH GAME HENS 🧳

makes 2 roasted game hens

When flattened, these game hens resemble an Italian trattoria classic, chicken under a brick. You'll need to start a few hours ahead, marinating the hens in the sauce for the best flavor. If you like, your butcher will gladly remove the backbone and flatten the hens for you. Serve this dish with a tossed salad of peaches and spring greens, dressed in a raspberry vinaigrette, or alongside a bed of arugula, dressed with some of the pan juices.

2 medium Cornish game hens (about 1 pound each), giblets removed, the hens rinsed under cold water
½ cup plus 1 tablespoon lemon juice
¼ cup olive oil
1 tablespoon red wine vinegar
1 small garlic clove, minced
2 teaspoons minced fresh rosemary, or 1 teaspoon minced dried rosemary
½ teaspoon salt
½ teaspoon freshly ground black pepper
3 tablespoons chopped fresh parsley, or 1 tablespoon dried parsley

1. To butcher the hens, place them breast side up on a clean, dry work surface. Insert a chef's knife blade down in one bird through the neck opening (i.e., the larger hole of the bird). The knife's tip should just touch the other end of the bird. Feel for the backbone below the knife blade, then cut down on one side of the backbone. Lift the blade slightly and cut down on the other side of the backbone, thereby cutting out the bone. Remove the knife from the hen and turn the bird breast side down on your work surface. Slide your hands inside the cavity through the opening where the backbone was; gently but firmly pry the hen open, flattening it with the heels of your hands. The wishbone may snap as you do this—if not, you'll need to break it as you flatten the bird. Now push the hen open even further, thereby cracking the

breastbone so that the bird can lie flat (thinking of it as cracking the spine of a book). Repeat with the second game hen.

2. Whisk the lemon juice, olive oil, vinegar, garlic, rosemary, salt, and pepper in a medium roasting pan or baking dish until well combined, but not until emulsified. Place both flattened game hens in this marinade, turning once to coat. Cover the baking dish with plastic wrap and refrigerate for at least 2 but no more than 4 hours, turning occasionally.

3. Preheat the broiler with the broiler rack 4 to 6 inches from the heat source. Remove the hens from the marinade and place them breast side down on the broiler rack. (You can cover the rack in aluminum foil to save a messy cleanup later on.) Broil for 12 minutes. Turn the birds breast side up and spoon some of the marinade over the top. Broil for an additional 8 minutes, or until the skin is golden brown and the juices run clear. Sprinkle each of the birds with half the parsley and serve.

TURKEY AND DRESSING

makes 1 stuffed boneless turkey breast,
or 2 servings

So what if it's not a whole turkey? It's a turkey breast cutlet, pounded thin and rolled around a cornbread stuffing.

2 tablespoons unsalted butter
1 medium shallot, minced
1 medium celery rib, minced
3 medium cremini mushrooms, cleaned and minced (about ⅔ cup)
1 tablespoon dry vermouth
1 purchased, day-old corn muffin (see Note)
One 14½-ounce can chicken stock (regular, low-fat, or nonfat, but preferably low-sodium)

1 large egg yolk, lightly beaten
1 teaspoon chopped fresh sage, or ½ teaspoon rubbed sage
1 teaspoon fresh thyme, or ½ teaspoon dried thyme
½ teaspoon salt
½ teaspoon freshly ground black pepper
One 14- to 16-ounce turkey breast cutlet
1 tablespoon olive oil
2 teaspoons all-purpose flour

1. To make the stuffing, melt 1 tablespoon of the butter in a medium saucepan set over medium heat. Add the shallot and celery; cook for 2 minutes, or until softened, stirring frequently. Stir in the mushrooms and continue cooking for about 4 minutes, or until they have given off their juices and the pan is again almost dry, stirring frequently. Pour in the vermouth and stir well to scrape up any browned bits on the bottom of the pan. Transfer the mixture to a medium bowl. Crumble in the purchased corn muffin, then stir in 3 tablespoons of the chicken stock, the egg yolk, sage, thyme, salt, and pepper. Mix well and set aside.

2. Lay a large sheet of plastic wrap on a clean, dry work surface, then place the turkey breast cutlet smooth side down on it. Open the breast out as far as possible, making shallow cuts in the meat to help open it further and further, especially at a thick or seemingly "doubled" part of the breast meat. The shallow cuts will allow the breast to open out as far as possible without any holes or tears in the meat. Cover with a second sheet of plastic wrap. Using a heavy saucepan or the smooth side of a meat mallet, pound the breast to about ½-inch thickness. Do not pound the meat so thin that holes form. Remove the top sheet of plastic wrap. If desired, you can have your butcher do this step for you; ask him or her to butterfly and pound the meat to ½-inch thickness.

3. Place the prepared stuffing in a compact oval in the middle of the pounded cutlet. Fold the two long sides of the breast cutlet over the stuffing to cover it. Use butcher twine to tie the cutlet closed, wrapping the "log" in two or three places. You can also tie off the ends, or wrap one piece of twine lengthwise around the entire cutlet, thereby securing the ends, so that the filling doesn't leak out while it bakes.

4. Melt the remaining 1 tablespoon of butter with the olive oil over medium-high heat in a pot just large enough to hold the stuffed cutlet. Add the turkey and cook for about 7 minutes, turning occasionally to brown all the outside surface. Add 1 cup of the chicken stock to the pan and bring it to a boil. Cover, reduce the heat to low, and braise the stuffed cutlet for 30 minutes, or until the meat is cooked through.

5. Remove the cutlet to a cutting board and tent with foil to keep warm. Raise the heat to high under the pan and bring the cooking liquid to a boil. Continue boiling for about 3 minutes, or until this mixture is a glaze, stirring occasionally. Meanwhile, whisk the remaining stock and flour in a small bowl. Once the cooking liquid has been reduced to a glaze, whisk this flour mixture into the pot; continue cooking and whisking for about 30 seconds, or until the mixture boils and thickens. Carve the stuffed cutlet into rings and serve with the thickened gravy.

> **NOTE:** One leftover corn muffin is enough for this stuffing. If you've bought one fresh, cut it into quarters, set them on a baking sheet, and bake them in a preheated 250°F oven for about 10 minutes, or until they're dry but not browned, turning occasionally.

SWEET-AND-SOUR POTATOES AND TURKEY

makes 2 servings

China is now the world's largest producer of potatoes—and so spuds have begun showing up in lots of dishes, particularly those from Szechwan, where the fiery flavors marry well with starchy potatoes. The potatoes are actually cooked until crisp, not until soft, a surprise texture that gives this dish a lot of crunch along with the heat. Add more crushed red pepper if you want a spicier dish. Since the potatoes are already starchy, serve this easy entrée with wilted greens or alongside a tossed salad, dressed with soy sauce and rice wine vinegar.

2 tablespoons water

1½ tablespoons rice vinegar (see page 12)

1 tablespoon sugar

2 teaspoons soy sauce (regular or low-sodium)

1 teaspoon tomato paste (see page 14)

¾ pound yellow-fleshed potatoes, such as Yukon Gold, peeled

1½ tablespoons peanut oil

1 large garlic clove, minced

2 teaspoons peeled, minced fresh ginger

¼ teaspoon red pepper flakes, or to taste

6 ounces turkey breast cutlet, or turkey scaloppini, sliced into matchsticks

1 small green bell pepper, cored, seeded, and chopped

1. To make the sweet-and-sour sauce, whisk the water, rice vinegar, sugar, soy sauce, and tomato paste in a small bowl until the sugar and tomato paste dissolve; set aside.

2. Shred the potatoes using the large holes of a box grater or a mandoline with the shoestring setting. Alternatively, use a Japanese cooking tool called Cook's Help, which will produce long threads of potatoes—these will need to be cut into 6- to 10-inch-long pieces. Place the shredded potatoes in a large bowl, cover with cold water, and let stand for 1 minute. Drain and squeeze dry to remove some of the excess starch. Set the shredded potatoes aside.

3. Heat a wok or medium sauté pan over medium-high heat. Swirl in the oil to coat the pan, then sauté the garlic, ginger, and red pepper flakes about 10 seconds, or until fragrant. Add the turkey and stir-fry about 30 seconds, or until it loses its raw, pink color. Stir in the bell pepper and stir-fry about 30 seconds, then add the potatoes. Toss and cook for 2 minutes, just until limp but still crunchy.

4. Pour the prepared sweet-and-sour sauce into the pan; stir-fry for 1 minute, or until the sauce comes to a simmer and is incorporated into the potato mixture. Serve at once.

PAN-SEARED DUCK BREASTS *with* HONEY AND FIGS 💼

makes **2 servings**

Elegant and flavorful, duck breasts are also surprisingly easy to prepare. Here, they're complemented with a delicate sauce of honey, vinegar, and fresh figs.

2 medium boneless duck breast fillets (about 10 ounces each)	½ cup dry vermouth
	1 teaspoon Champagne vinegar or white wine vinegar
½ teaspoon freshly ground black pepper	2 teaspoons honey, preferably a very aromatic honey such as wildflower, thistle, or pine
¼ teaspoon salt	
1 medium shallot, minced	
½ teaspoon fresh thyme, or ¼ teaspoon dried thyme	3 fresh figs, stemmed and quartered (see Note)
1 small garlic clove, minced	

1. Position the rack in the middle of the oven and preheat the oven to 350°F. Score the skin and fat in the breasts with a paring knife to create a crosshatch pattern with ½-inch squares; season the breasts with the pepper and salt.

2. Heat a large, oven-safe skillet, preferably cast-iron, over high heat until it is smoking. Add the duck breasts skin side down and immediately reduce the heat to low. Cook for 6 minutes, or until golden. You may need to shake the pan vigorously once or twice to keep the breasts from sticking. Turn and cook for an additional 3 minutes.

3. Place the skillet in the oven and roast for about 6 minutes, or until an instant-read thermometer inserted halfway into the thickest part of the breast registers 130°F (for medium-rare, the preferred doneness); or for about 8 minutes, to 140°F for medium.

4. Transfer the duck breasts to a plate; tent with foil to keep warm. Pour off all but 1 tablespoon of the rendered duck fat in the skillet. Place the skillet over medium-low heat. Add the shallot and thyme; cook for 2 minutes, or until the shallot is softened and the mixture is very fragrant, stirring constantly. Stir in the garlic, cook for just 10 seconds, then pour in the vermouth and vinegar. Raise the heat to high and bring the mixture to a boil, scraping up any browned bits on the bottom of the pan. Boil for 1 minute, stirring constantly, until reduced by half.

5. Swirl in the honey and cook for about 10 seconds, just until the honey melts, stirring constantly. Add the figs and cook for 10 more seconds, just until heated through. Remove the sauce from the heat.

6. To serve, slice the duck breasts into ¼-inch-thick slices. Arrange them on two plates, then divide the sauce between the two servings. Serve immediately.

> **NOTE:** Fresh figs are delicate and sweet—but often hard to find. You can substitute 3 dried Black Mission figs, soaked in hot water for 15 minutes, until soft and plump, then drained, stemmed, and quartered.

Pork *and* Lamb

Pork and lamb lend themselves to complex but bright flavors, even in small batches. Here, we've set them against an international palate of tastes, substantial fare for any night of the week. There are some easy sautés using boneless pork chops, an elegant rack of lamb for two, and even a recipe for oven-barbecued baby back ribs.

SAUTÉED PORK CUTLETS *with* GREEN PEPPERCORN SAUCE ⏱

makes **2 servings**

Green peppercorns are soft, underripe peppercorn berries. They're available packed in oil (in which case they should be drained and rinsed for this dish), packed in water (in which case they should simply be drained), or freeze-dried. Look for firm, whole peppercorns, each berry vibrant green, not dusty brown. Serve these pork chops and their aromatic sauce alongside baked potatoes, an acorn squash purée, or buttered noodles tossed with poppy seeds.

Four 3-ounce boneless pork loin cutlets, each about ½ inch thick

¼ teaspoon salt

¼ teaspoon freshly ground black pepper

1 tablespoon olive oil

1 small shallot, minced

1 small garlic clove, minced

1½ teaspoons green peppercorns, lightly crushed with the side of a knife or in a mortar with a pestle

½ cup dry vermouth

2 tablespoons White Worcestershire sauce (see Note)

1 tablespoon unsalted butter, at room temperature

1. Season the pork chops with salt and pepper. Heat a large skillet or sauté pan, preferably a nonstick or cast-iron pan, over medium-high heat. Swirl in the oil, then slip the chops into the pan. Cook for 5 minutes, then turn them with tongs or a fork. If the oil begins to smoke, reduce the heat to medium. Add the shallot, garlic, and green peppercorns; continue cooking for 3 minutes, stirring occasionally so the vegetables don't stick.

2. Pour in the vermouth and bring the mixture to a boil. Boil for 1 minute, then stir in the White Worcestershire sauce. Simmer for 30 seconds, just to reduce slightly, then swirl in the butter, stirring just until it's melted and incorporated into the sauce. Serve immediately.

N O T E : White Worcestershire sauce is sometimes labeled "Worcestershire for Chicken." It's a lighter blend, made with Sauterne, a sweet wine. Don't substitute regular Worcestershire sauce, which is too thick and will overpower the peppercorns in this dish. If you can't find White Worcestershire, substitute 1½ tablespoons dry sherry, ½ teaspoon cider vinegar, ¼ teaspoon sugar, and ¼ teaspoon salt, mixed together before being added to the sauce.

SAUTÉED PORK CUTLETS
with MUSTARD SAUCE

makes 2 servings

With its tangy sour cream and mustard sauce, this easy pork sauté is best served with plain noodles or white rice. If you can't find thin boneless pork cutlets, ask your butcher to butterfly two 1-inch-thick loin chops for you; press them open along their "hinge" or seam to flatten them out before you sauté them.

Four 3-ounce boneless pork loin cutlets, each about ½ inch thick
½ teaspoon freshly ground black pepper
¼ teaspoon salt
2 tablespoons unsalted butter, at room temperature, or 2 tablespoons olive oil

1 small shallot, minced
½ teaspoon caraway seeds
¼ cup dry vermouth
2 teaspoons Dijon mustard
2 tablespoons sour cream

1. Season the cutlets with pepper and salt and set them aside. Heat a medium skillet or sauté pan over medium heat, then add 1 tablespoon of the butter or the oil. Slip the cutlets into the pan and cook for about 4 minutes, or until lightly browned. Turn and cook for about 3 more minutes, or until cooked through and golden. Transfer to two dinner plates and tent with foil to keep warm.

2. Return the pan to medium heat and add the remaining 1 tablespoon of the butter or oil. Stir in the shallot and caraway seeds; cook for about 1 minute, or until the shallot has softened. Pour in the vermouth, raise the heat to medium-high, and bring the mixture to a simmer. Cook for just 20 seconds, until the vermouth is slightly reduced, then whisk in the mustard until smooth. Remove the pan from the heat and whisk in the sour cream. Set the pan aside for 30 seconds, to heat the sour cream, then divide this sauce between the cutlets and serve immediately.

SMOKED PORK
CHOPS WITH APPLES

makes **2 servings**

This is an easy dinner, perfect for a chilly night. The apples mellow the sauerkraut considerably, giving the dish a sweet, light taste. Don't use lip-puckering canned sauerkraut. Buy it fresh in small packages from your butcher, or in the deli case at your market. Or buy it directly from your neighborhood deli, in exactly the amount you need.

One 8-ounce package fresh
    sauerkraut, drained
2 medium apples (about
    4 ounces each), preferably
    Jonathans or Northern
    Spys, peeled, cored, and
    thinly sliced
1 tablespoon Dijon mustard

1 teaspoon caraway seeds
6 tablespoons apple juice
2 large smoked pork chops,
    about 8 ounces each
    (see Note)
4 to 6 small red-skinned
    potatoes, scrubbed

1. Mix the sauerkraut, apples, mustard, and caraway seeds in a large skillet or sauté pan, preferably nonstick or cast-iron. Stir in the apple juice, then place the skillet over medium-high heat and bring the mixture to a simmer.

2. Nestle the pork chops and potatoes in the pan. Cover, reduce the heat to low, and simmer for 35 minutes, until the liquid has thickened, the chops are heated through, and the potatoes are tender when pierced with a fork. Serve immediately.

NOTE: Smoked pork chops are available at deli counters, or in gourmet markets. Pink smoked chops have been doped with nitrates to keep them that color. If you prefer nitrate-free chops, look for ones that are light brown, maybe somewhat gray. The latter are also probably available from your local barbecue restaurant or smokehouse.

Variations

Substitute a large pear (about 7 ounces) for the apple.

Substitute apple brandy for the apple juice.

Add 2 tablespoons golden raisins or currants to the sauerkraut mixture with the caraway seeds.

Substitute a medium turnip or rutabaga (about 6 ounces), cut into quarters, for the potatoes; nestle these into the sauerkraut mixture with the chops.

OVEN-BARBECUED RIBS

makes 1 rack of baby back ribs

The trick to oven-barbecuing ribs is to roast them in a low-heat oven for a very long time. First, coat the ribs with the dry spice rub, then let them marinate in the refrigerator; you can even rub them the night before and fix them the next day. Once they're in the oven, be patient—wait until the meat is falling off the bone but still juicy, not until it has dried out. Serve these ribs with your favorite barbecue sauce on the side.

2 teaspoons packed light
   brown sugar
2 teaspoons chili powder
2 teaspoons mild paprika
1 teaspoon salt
½ teaspoon dry mustard
½ teaspoon ground cumin

½ teaspoon dried thyme
   (do not use fresh)
¼ teaspoon freshly ground
   black pepper
One 2-pound rack of baby back
   pork ribs (12 to 14 bones;
   see Note)

1. Mix the brown sugar, chili powder, paprika, salt, dry mustard, cumin, thyme, and pepper in a small bowl until well combined. Pat this mixture onto the ribs, taking care to massage it gently into the meat. Wrap the ribs in foil or plastic wrap and refrigerate for at least 2 hours or up to 24 hours.

2. Position the rack in the middle of the oven and preheat the oven to 275°F. Take the ribs out of the refrigerator and let them return to room temperature.

3. Place the ribs meat side down on the baking rack set in a broiler pan, or on a wire rack set on a large, lipped baking sheet. Bake for 30 minutes, then turn and continue baking for 1½ hours, or until the meat has pulled back from the bones and is tender between them. If the meat is still not fork-tender, cook for up to 30 more minutes. Serve with your favorite barbecue sauce as a dipping sauce.

> NOTE: Some baby back ribs have a thin, tough membrane on the bone side of the rack. Peel off this paper-like covering before rubbing the ribs with the spice mixture. Or ask your butcher to peel it off for you.

SPICE-RUBBED PORK TENDERLOIN WITH CHILE BEANS

♈♈

makes 2 servings

Here, a lean pork tenderloin is marinated in southwestern spices and broiled, then served alongside spicy beans. The only thing else you need? Lemon sorbet doused with vodka for dessert.

3 tablespoons olive oil
1 tablespoon Worcestershire sauce
2 teaspoons liquid smoke, optional
1 teaspoon ground cumin
¼ teaspoon salt
One ¾-pound pork tenderloin, trimmed
1 ancho chile (see page 8), halved and seeded
1 large ear of corn
1 tablespoon unsalted butter, at room temperature
1 small onion, chopped
¼ cup chopped dried apple

One 15-ounce can mixed beans, or red kidney beans, drained and rinsed
1 large Italian plum tomato, chopped
3 tablespoons chopped fresh chives; or 1 medium scallion, green part only, minced
One 14½-ounce can chicken stock (regular, low-fat, or nonfat, but preferably low-sodium)
¼ teaspoon salt, or to taste
¼ teaspoon freshly ground black pepper

1. Mix the olive oil, Worcestershire sauce, liquid smoke (if using), cumin, and salt in a resealable plastic bag large enough to hold the meat until a thin paste forms. Add the pork tenderloin, seal, and shake to coat the pork with the paste. Refrigerate for at least 2 hours but for no more than 12 hours, shaking the bag once in a while to recoat the tenderloin in the spice mixture. Alternatively, place the tenderloin in a small shallow baking dish, pour the spice mixture over, then turn to coat; cover with plastic wrap and refrigerate as directed, turning the tenderloin in the marinade at least twice.

2. Toast the seeded ancho halves in a clean, dry skillet set over medium-high heat for 2 minutes, or until very fragrant, turning once. Be careful—the oils will volatilize and can burn your eyes. Remove the chile from the pan, finely chop it, then set it aside.

3. Brown the ear of corn over an open gas flame, holding it with a pair of tongs; or place it on a baking sheet 4 to 6 inches below a preheated broiler. The kernels may pop, so stand back. Once the ear is lightly browned, slice off the kernels and set them aside, discarding the cob.

4. Melt the butter in a medium saucepan set over medium heat. Add the onion and cook for 3 minutes, or until golden, stirring frequently. Add the chopped chile, the reserved corn kernels, and the dried apple. Continue cooking for about 2 minutes, or just until the apples pieces soften; then stir in the beans, tomato, and chives. Cook for 30 seconds, stirring constantly, then pour in the stock. Bring the mixture to a boil, scraping up any browned bits in the pan; then reduce the heat to low and simmer, uncovered, for about 30 minutes, or until thickened, stirring often to avoid sticking.

5. Meanwhile, preheat the broiler. Place the reserved pork tenderloin on a lipped baking sheet or the broiler rack set 4 to 6 inches from the heat source. You can cover either pan with aluminum foil to ease cleanup. Broil for 6 minutes, turn, then broil for 6 more minutes, or until browned and an instant-read thermometer inserted into the thickest part of the tenderloin reads 155°F. Remove from the broiler and tent with foil. Let stand at room temperature before carving.

6. To serve, season the bean mixture with salt and pepper. Slice the tenderloin into ¼-inch rounds. Divide the bean mixture between two plates, mounding it in the center of each; top each with half the pork slices. Serve immediately.

CHINESE MINCED PORK AND SOUR BEANS

makes **2 servings**

This Szechwan classic is a vinegary, fiery farrago of long beans and pork. Choose Chinese long beans that are dull green, without withered edges or brown spots. Serve this entrée over white or brown rice, noodles of any variety, or wilted greens.

2 cups rice vinegar (see page 12)

⅓ pound Chinese long beans, trimmed and sliced into ¼-inch pieces (about 1½ cups), or ⅓ pound green beans, trimmed and cut into ¼-inch pieces

2 tablespoons peanut oil

2 medium garlic cloves, minced

1 tablespoon peeled, minced fresh ginger

1 teaspoon red pepper flakes

½ pound ground pork

2 tablespoons soy sauce (regular or low-sodium)

1. Bring the vinegar to a boil in a medium saucepan set over medium-high heat. Add the beans, cover the pan, and cook for 2 minutes. Drain the beans in a colander set in the sink, but do not rinse them.

2. Heat the oil in a wok or medium high-sided sauté pan set over medium-high heat. Add the garlic, ginger, and red pepper flakes; stir-fry for 1 minute, tossing constantly. Crumble in the ground pork and stir-fry for 4 minutes, tossing constantly. Add the beans and cook for 1 minute. Stir in the soy sauce, cook for an additional 30 seconds, and serve.

LAMB-STUFFED BELL PEPPERS 🧳

makes **2 stuffed peppers**

Here's a Greek twist on the family classic, with pine nuts, dill, and ground lamb. Choose bell peppers of any color but with wide bottoms, preferably in four well-defined lobes, which will help them stand up in the saucepan while they're baking.

2 tablespoons pine nuts

¾ pound ground lamb

1 medium shallot, minced

3 tablespoons chopped fresh dill, or 1 tablespoon dried dill

3 tablespoons white rice

2 tablespoons currants

1 teaspoon tomato paste (see page 14)

1 tablespoon chopped fresh parsley, or 1 teaspoon dried parsley

1 teaspoon grated lemon zest

½ teaspoon salt

½ teaspoon freshly ground black pepper

2 large bell peppers (about 8 ounces each)

One 8-ounce can tomato sauce

¼ cup water

1 tablespoon olive oil

½ teaspoon lemon juice

1. Position the oven rack in the middle of the oven and preheat the oven to 350°F. Meanwhile, toast the pine nuts in a small, dry skillet set over low heat for about 4 minutes, or until lightly browned, tossing frequently. Set them aside.

2. Mix the lamb, shallot, and 2 tablespoons of the fresh dill or 2 teaspoons of the dried dill in a large bowl with a fork, just until the shallot and dill are combined into the meat. Gently mix in the toasted pine nuts, the rice, currants, tomato paste, parsley, ½ teaspoon of the lemon zest, salt, and pepper until combined. Take care not to mix until the meat fibers begin to break down.

3. Cut the tops of the peppers by slicing down about ¼ inch below the stem. Using a small spoon, preferably a grapefruit spoon, scoop out the seeds and inner membranes but take care not to scrape the walls and thereby weaken the pepper's structure. Stuff each pepper with half of the lamb mixture. Place the stuffed peppers in a 2-quart saucepan or pot. Set aside.

4. Mix the tomato sauce, water, olive oil, lemon juice, the remaining dill, and the remaining ½ teaspoon of lemon zest in a medium bowl; pour this mixture over the stuffed peppers. Place the saucepan over medium heat and bring the mixture to a boil. Cover and place the pan in the oven. Bake for 45 minutes. Uncover and bake for an additional 15 minutes, until the sauce thickens and the peppers are tender. Let stand for 5 minutes off the heat before serving.

TEA-RUBBED RACK OF LAMB with ROASTED POTATOES 🍷🍷

makes 1 rack of lamb

We've infused a rack of lamb with green tea—it mellows the meat considerably while keeping it moist and flavorful. For even better flavor, coat the rack in the morning, then leave it covered in the refrigerator all day. Take the lamb out of the refrigerator 15 minutes before roasting, so it can return to room temperature.

1 tablespoon green tea leaves, ground to a powder in a spice grinder or with a mortar and pestle; or 1 tablespoon powdered green tea (but not instant green tea)

2 teaspoons ground coriander

1 teaspoon salt

One 1-pound rack of lamb (7 or 8 bones), frenched (see Note)

2 tablespoons canola or other vegetable oil

1 pound red-skinned potatoes, the smallest you can find

1. Mix the tea, ground coriander, and ½ teaspoon of the salt in a small bowl. Rub the lamb meat with 1 tablespoon of the oil, then massage the tea mixture into the meat. You needn't coat the bones. Place the herbed rack in a shallow roasting pan or baking dish, cover with plastic wrap, and refrigerate for at least 4 hours, or preferably for 12 hours, but for no more than 24 hours. Bring the lamb back to room temperature before continuing with the recipe.

2. Position the rack in the middle of the oven and preheat the oven to 350°F. Bring a medium pot of water to a boil over high heat. Add the potatoes and boil for 5 minutes, or just until they begin to soften on the outside but still have a firm inner core. Drain and immediately toss with the remaining 1 tablespoon of oil and ½ teaspoon of salt.

3. Heat a flame-proof roasting pan or a high-sided, oven-safe medium sauté pan over medium heat. Add the rack of lamb and brown it on all sides for 3 minutes, turning as necessary. Scatter the potatoes around the pan, then place it in the oven.

4. Bake for about 20 minutes for rare, turning the potatoes once, until the lamb registers 125°F when an instant-read thermometer is inserted in the thickest part of the meat without touching a bone. For medium-rare, add 3 minutes and roast to 130°F; for medium, add 8 minutes and roast to 140°F. Do not roast lamb to temperatures above 140°F or it will turn leathery. Allow the rack to stand at room temperature for 5 minutes before carving between the bones and separating the chops to serve.

> **NOTE:** A frenched rack has had the fat, cartilage, and some of the meat pulled back from the ribs themselves, thereby separating them and leaving a round "eye" of meat along the bottom of the bones. In the United States, most racks of lamb are sold frenched. If for some reason yours isn't, slice between the bones to the rounded eye of meat, then clear away the material between the bones by shaving it off the bone, being careful not to splinter the bones as you pull your knife across them. Or ask your butcher to french the rack for you.

Elegant Potatoes

Substitute 1 pound large, peeled, yellow-fleshed potatoes, such as Yukon Gold, for the red-skinned potatoes. Use a melon baller to scoop perfectly rounded balls out of the flesh. There is some waste, but the final presentation is quite dramatic. In fact, you can use this technique for any recipe that calls for small "new" potatoes.

Beef *and* Veal

Of all the things we're likely to give up when we're cooking in small batches, beef is surely at the top of the list. But there's no reason it needs to be. Sure, steaks make an easy dinner for two. But most any beef dish, from hamburgers to rib roast, can be made for two: just buy a lean cut, add a few pantry staples, and dinner's on the table in no time.

INSIDE-OUT CHEESEBURGERS

makes **2 stuffed patties**

If you put the cheese inside the hamburger patty, it infuses the meat—and it won't drip all over the grill or the frying pan. Serve these burgers on the buns of your choice along with your favorite condiments.

¾ pound lean ground beef
1 teaspoon Worcestershire
    sauce
½ teaspoon freshly ground
    black pepper
2 tablespoons shredded
    Cheddar (about ½ ounce)
2 tablespoons freshly grated
    Parmigiano-Reggiano
    (about ½ ounce)

½ teaspoon caraway seeds,
    lightly crushed in a spice
    grinder or in a mortar with
    a pestle
1 tablespoon canola or other
    vegetable oil

1. Gently mix the ground beef, Worcestershire sauce, and pepper in a medium bowl with your hands or a wooden spoon; do not mix until the meat fibers break down. Divide the mixture into four balls, each about 4 inches in diameter; pat each into a ¼-inch-thick patty.

2. In a separate bowl, mix the Cheddar, Parmigiano-Reggiano, and crushed caraway seeds. Place half this mixture in the center of each of two patties; cover each of these patties with one of the remaining patties. Press the edges to seal closed.

3. Heat a large skillet or sauté pan, preferably cast-iron, over high heat until smoking. Swirl in the oil, then slip the patties into the pan. Cook for 4 minutes, turning once, for medium doneness; or cook for 6 minutes, turning once, for well-done. Transfer the patties to a carving board; let rest for 5 minutes before serving. Alternatively, oil the grill grate, then heat the grill according to the manufacturer's instructions.

Cook the patties over high heat or 4 to 6 inches above high-heat coals for about 6 minutes, or until cooked through, turning once. Serve on your choice of bun or roll.

Cheese Shop Burgers
Omit the cheese in the recipe and replace with any one of these combinations:

> 2 tablespoons grated Gruyère and 2 tablespoons grated Emmenthaler
> 2 tablespoons grated Havarti and 2 tablespoons grated Asiago
> 2 tablespoons grated smoked Gouda and 2 tablespoons grated Brie (the Brie must be very cold to grate)
> 2 tablespoons crumbled Gorgonzola and 2 tablespoons grated Swiss
> 2 tablespoons crumbled Tellegio and 2 tablespoons grated Manchego

CHUTNEY-GLAZED MEATLOAF

makes 1 small meatloaf

Meatloaf is one thing you might never consider making when you cook for two, but here's a cut-down, souped-up version that may be just the ticket. It's made with toasted almonds, dried apple, Eastern spices, and bread crumbs, then topped with a tangy chutney glaze.

1 tablespoon sliced blanched almonds	¾ teaspoon salt
2 tablespoons canola or other vegetable oil	¼ cup plain dried bread crumbs
1 small shallot, minced	1 medium egg, lightly beaten, or 3 tablespoons pasteurized egg substitute, such as Egg Beaters
1 small garlic clove, minced	
2 teaspoons peeled, minced fresh ginger	1 pound lean ground beef
¼ cup chopped dried apple	3 tablespoons mango chutney, melted (see Note)
1 medium celery rib, minced	
1½ teaspoons curry powder	

1. Position the oven rack in the middle of the oven and preheat the oven to 350°F. Toast the almonds on a baking sheet for about 5 minutes, or until lightly browned, stirring occasionally. Transfer to a small bowl and set aside; maintain the oven's temperature.

2. Heat a medium skillet or sauté pan over medium heat. Swirl in the oil, then add the shallot, garlic, and ginger. Cook for just 30 seconds, or until the ginger becomes fragrant, stirring constantly. Stir in the apple and celery; soften for about 3 minutes. Sprinkle the curry powder and salt over the mixture and stir well. Transfer to a medium bowl and cool for about 5 minutes, or until easy to handle, stirring a few times.

3. Meanwhile, use a fork to mix the bread crumbs and egg in a small bowl until moist and uniform. Pour this mixture into the prepared vegetables, then crumble in the ground beef. Mix together, preferably with your hands, or with a wooden spoon. Do not break up the meat fibers, but make sure the vegetables and bread crumbs are well incorporated throughout. Form this mixture into a small, oblong mound and place it in the center of a nonstick baking sheet, or a regular baking sheet lined with either parchment paper or a silicon baking sheet. Spread the melted chutney over the top and sides of the meatloaf.

4. Bake for about 45 minutes, or until the glaze is set and the meatloaf is cooked through, or until an instant-read thermometer inserted halfway into the thickest part of the loaf registers 150°F for medium, 160°F for well-done. Cooking this meatloaf to rare or medium-rare is not recommended because of the raw eggs in the filling. Remove from the oven and sprinkle the top with the sliced almonds. Let stand for 5 minutes before serving.

> **NOTE:** To melt the chutney, place it in a small saucepan set over low heat and stir for about 1 minute. Or place it in a small bowl and microwave on high for 30 seconds, then stir until fully melted. Substitute any chutney you like except one with nuts, which may burn during the meatloaf's long roasting.

SWEDISH MEATBALLS

makes **2 servings**

With a touch of sour cream and ground spices, these meatballs are certainly more than just a cocktail appetizer to be served with toothpicks! Serve them any night on their own, on top of noodles, or alongside mashed potatoes. If you can't find ground veal, use all ground beef.

⅓ pound lean ground beef
⅓ pound ground veal
1 large egg yolk, at room temperature
2 medium shallots, minced
3 tablespoons plain dried bread crumbs
2 tablespoons milk or 2 tablespoons heavy cream
¾ teaspoon salt
½ teaspoon grated nutmeg
½ teaspoon freshly ground black pepper

1 tablespoon all-purpose flour
¼ teaspoon ground allspice
⅛ teaspoon ground cloves
One 14½-ounce can beef stock (regular, low-fat, or nonfat, but preferably low-sodium)
2 tablespoons unsalted butter, at room temperature
2 tablespoons sour cream (regular, low-fat, or nonfat)

1. In a medium bowl, mix the ground beef and veal with a fork just until combined. Mix in the egg yolk, shallots, bread crumbs, milk, ½ teaspoon of the salt, nutmeg, and ¼ teaspoon of the pepper just until combined, but not so much that the meat fibers break apart into mush. Form this mixture by tablespoonfuls into 20 or so balls; set them aside.

2. In a small bowl, mix the flour with the remaining ¼ teaspoon of salt, the remaining ¼ teaspoon of pepper, the allspice, and cloves; set aside. To concentrate its flavors, bring the beef stock to a boil in a small saucepan set over high heat. Boil for about 5 minutes, or until reduced to 1 cup. Set aside, covered, to keep warm.

3. Melt the butter in a large skillet or sauté pan set over medium heat. Add the meatballs and sauté for about 4 minutes, or until browned, turning occasionally. Use a fine-mesh sieve or strainer to sift the prepared flour and spice mixture over the meatballs. Shake the skillet once or twice to mix any flour with the fat in the pan (stirring the mixture can break up the meatballs). Continue cooking for 1 minute, shaking the pan frequently; then pour in the reduced stock. Again, shake the pan a few times to combine the stock and the flour and to distribute the mixture evenly. Reduce the heat to low and simmer, uncovered, for 10 minutes, basting the meatballs often with the sauce. Stir in the sour cream, cover, and immediately remove the pan from the heat. Let stand for 5 minutes before serving.

KOREAN BEEF KABOBS

makes **2 skewers**

We've recreated the traditional sesame-flavored Korean kabob by using lean sirloin steak, a cut more readily available and certainly less fatty than the beef shoulder traditionally used in this staple of Korean street food. You can deepen the flavors by marinating the steak all day. All you need is brown rice and some steamed green beans for a complete meal.

2 tablespoons soy sauce

1 tablespoon red wine vinegar

1 tablespoon sesame oil

1 tablespoon packed light brown sugar

1½ teaspoons peeled, minced fresh ginger

1 teaspoon mild paprika

1 teaspoon red chili paste (see page 12)

½ teaspoon freshly ground black pepper

1 small shallot, minced

1 small garlic clove, minced

¾ pound sirloin steak, trimmed, cut into 1-inch cubes

1 medium green bell pepper, cored, seeded, and cut into 1-inch strips (about 6 pieces)

1 small red onion, cut into quarters (see Notes)

Two 8- to 10-inch bamboo skewers, soaked in water at least 20 minutes (see Notes)

1. Whisk the soy sauce, vinegar, sesame oil, brown sugar, ginger, paprika, red chili paste, black pepper, shallot, and garlic in a large bowl until the sugar dissolves. Add the cubed steak and toss to coat. Cover and refrigerate for at least 2 hours but no more than 12 hours, tossing occasionally.

2. Preheat the broiler, placing the broiler rack or oven rack 4 to 6 inches from the heat source. Drain the meat, reserving the marinade. Thread the meat, green pepper strips, and onion quarters onto the soaked skewers, alternating meat and vegetables. Wrap the ends of the skewers in small pieces of aluminum foil. You can also line a lipped baking sheet or the broiler pan with aluminum foil to facilitate cleanup afterward.

3. Place the kabobs on a broiler pan or a lipped baking sheet. Broil for 8 minutes, basting occasionally with the reserved marinade and turning once, until the meat is cooked through and the vegetables begin to brown. Serve immediately.

> NOTES: To keep the onion layers together after the onion is quartered, do not slice off the root end before peeling and quartering the onion. Make sure each cut goes through the root, thereby taking a small piece of the root end into each quarter, allowing it to stay together.
>
> We do not recommend metal skewers for this dish, because they heat the steak from the inside, thereby overcooking it.

HAWAIIAN STEAKS

The sauce for these strip steaks was inspired by teriyaki sauce, that sweet but salty Japanese classic. Make sure you use pineapple chunks packed in juice, not syrup—the latter would be far too sweet. Rice pilaf would be a great accompaniment. You could use this same technique for boneless, skinless chicken breasts or boneless pork chops, either pounded thin. Or substitute two large, sliced portobello mushrooms for a quick vegetarian sauté.

Two 6-ounce strip steaks, trimmed	1 tablespoon olive oil
1/2 teaspoon freshly ground black pepper	1 tablespoon unsalted butter, at room temperature
2 tablespoons soy sauce (regular or low-sodium)	1 bell pepper, stemmed, cored, seeded, and cut into 1-inch pieces
1 tablespoon honey	One 8-ounce can pineapple chunks in juice, drained (about 1 cup)
1 tablespoon water	
1/2 teaspoon ground ginger	

1. Place a large sheet of plastic wrap on your work surface, lay the steaks on top of it about 4 inches apart, and cover with a second large sheet of plastic wrap. Pound the steaks to a 1/2-inch thickness with the smooth side of a meat mallet or the bottom of a heavy saucepan. Remove the plastic wrap, season the steaks with pepper, and set aside.

2. Whisk the soy sauce, honey, water, and ginger in a small bowl until smooth; set aside.

3. Heat a large skillet or sauté pan over medium heat; add the olive oil and butter. Once the butter has melted, slip the steaks into the pan and cook for 3 minutes, or until lightly browned. Turn and cook about 2 more minutes for rare, 3 for medium-rare, or 4 for medium. Do not cook pounded steaks for longer periods, or they will be tough. Cook the steaks one at a time if your skillet is not large enough to hold them both. Transfer the steaks to two dinner plates and tent with foil to keep warm.

4. Raise the heat under the pan to high; add the green pepper and pineapple chunks. Cook for about 3 minutes, or until the pepper begins to soften. Stir in the prepared soy sauce mixture and bring to a simmer, scraping up any browned bits on the bottom of the pan. Cook for about 1 minute, until slightly reduced, then pour over the prepared steaks and serve.

STEAK AU POIVRE

makes **2 servings**

Here's the bistro classic: steaks rubbed with cracked pepper, then served with a light cream sauce. The secret? Use a well-seasoned, cast-iron skillet; set it over high heat for 5 minutes, or until it's smoking, before adding the steaks. The outsides will caramelize into a crust before you roast the steaks in a very hot oven. Let the steaks rest for 5 minutes before serving, so that the juices reincorporate into the meat and the fibers relax. Do not use a nonstick skillet for this technique, since the high temperature can ruin the finish.

Two 8-ounce strip steaks, trimmed	2 teaspoons unsalted butter, at room temperature
1 tablespoon cracked black peppercorns (see Note)	1 medium shallot, chopped
¼ teaspoon salt	¼ cup brandy
1 tablespoon olive oil	2 tablespoons heavy cream
	¼ teaspoon grated nutmeg

1. Position the rack in the bottom third of the oven and preheat the oven to 475°F. Coat the steaks with the cracked peppercorns, pressing them into the meat. Season with salt; set aside.

2. Heat a well-seasoned cast-iron skillet over high heat for 5 minutes, or until smoking. Swirl in the oil, then add the coated steaks. Cook for 2 minutes, turning once.

3. Place the skillet in the oven—be careful: the pan is very hot—and cook for 4 minutes for rare, 6 minutes for medium-rare, or 8 minutes for medium. An instant-read thermometer inserted into the thickest part of one of the steaks should register 120°F for rare, 125°F for medium-rare, or 130°F for medium. Transfer the steaks to a serving platter or two dinner plates, tent with foil, and set aside.

4. Return the skillet to medium-high heat on the stove and swirl in the butter. Add the shallot and cook for 1 minute, or until quite browned, stirring constantly. Add the brandy and cook for 30 seconds, scraping up any browned bits on the bottom of the pan. The brandy may flame—if it does, cover the skillet and remove it from the heat for 30 seconds, or until the flame is out. Continue cooking until the brandy is reduced by half, then whisk in the cream and nutmeg. Bring the mixture to a boil, whisking constantly. Boil for 1 minute, or until reduced to a thick sauce. Pour over the steaks and serve.

NOTE: Use a mortar and pestle to crack the peppercorns; or place them between sheets of plastic wrap, fold the edges to seal, and hammer them with the smooth side of a meat mallet or the bottom of a heavy saucepan. You can use a mix of peppercorns in this dish: black, pink, green, and white.

STEAKS WITH MUSHROOM SAUCE

makes **2 servings**

Dried porcinis make a nice foil to tender, flavorful ribeyes. You may need to work in two pans to hold both the steaks, or use an extra-large sauté pan. Have everything ready before you start cooking because this dish comes together very quickly. Serve these steaks with the classic side: potatoes—baked, roasted, or mashed.

3 tablespoons dried porcini
¼ cup boiling water
Two 7-ounce ribeye steaks,
   trimmed
¼ teaspoon salt
¼ teaspoon freshly grated
   black pepper
1 tablespoon olive oil
2 teaspoons unsalted butter, at
   room temperature

1 small shallot, minced
1 small garlic clove, minced
1 teaspoon fresh thyme, or
   ½ teaspoon dried thyme
2 tablespoons dry vermouth
1 teaspoon red wine vinegar
¼ teaspoon sugar
3 tablespoons heavy cream

1. Place the porcinis in a small bowl and cover with the boiling water; set aside to soak for 15 minutes. Meanwhile, position the rack in the middle of the oven and preheat the oven to 475°F. Season the steaks with salt and pepper; set aside.

2. Drain the porcinis, reserving the soaking liquid. If the liquid is sandy, strain it through a chinoise or a fine-mesh strainer lined with cheesecloth.

3. Heat a well-seasoned cast-iron skillet over high heat until smoking. Swirl in the oil, then add the seasoned steaks. Cook for 3 minutes, turning once.

4. Place the skillet in the oven and cook for about 3 minutes for rare, 5 minutes for medium-rare, or 7 minutes for medium. An instant-read thermometer inserted into the thickest part of one of the steaks should register 120°F for rare, 125°F for medium-rare, or 130°F for medium. Transfer the steaks to a serving platter or two dinner plates, tent with foil, and set aside.

5. Return the skillet to medium-high heat on top of the stove and swirl in the butter. Add the shallot, garlic, thyme, and the soaked porcinis; cook for 1 minute, stirring constantly. Stir in the vermouth, vinegar, sugar, and the reserved mushroom soaking liquid; boil for 1 minute, or until reduced by half, stirring constantly. Pour in the cream. Boil for 1 minute, or until reduced to a thick sauce. Pour over the steaks and serve.

RIB ROAST FOR TWO

makes one 1-bone rib roast

Who could believe a rib roast for two? And who could believe how fast you can make it? It's so easy: just coat it in kosher salt and pepper and roast for under 20 minutes. Voilà, dinner in no time. Ask your butcher to give you a one-bone roast—not the so-called first bone, because it will be too lean to stand up to cooking as a thin, small roast; and not the last bone either, the one that's mostly fat. Ask for one of the bones somewhere in the middle of the ribs, about where the cut is made for the three- or four-bone roasts.

2 teaspoons olive oil
One 2-pound, 1-bone rib roast
½ teaspoon salt, preferably
   kosher salt
½ teaspoon freshly ground
   black pepper
1 small shallot, minced

1 small garlic clove, minced
1 teaspoon chopped fresh
   rosemary, or ½ teaspoon
   chopped dried rosemary
2 tablespoons brandy
1 teaspoon unsalted butter, at
   room temperature, optional

1. Position the rack in the middle of the oven and preheat the oven to 450°F. Massage the olive oil into the rib roast, then rub the salt and pepper into it.

2. Heat a large ovenproof skillet, preferably cast-iron, over high heat for about 4 minutes, or until smoking. Add the roast on its side and sear it for 2 minutes, turning once. Sear it on the top and bottom as well, about 30 seconds for each. Then place the skillet in the oven. Roast for about 16 minutes for rare, or 18 minutes for medium-rare, or until an instant-read thermometer inserted in the thickest part of the roast registers between 115°F and 120°F for rare or 125°F for medium-rare. Add about 3 additional minutes for medium (and an internal temperature of 130°F), or about 7 additional minutes for medium-well (140°F). Carefully remove the skillet from the oven—it is very hot—

then transfer the roast to a carving board and tent it with foil. The internal temperature of the roast will rise five to ten degrees as it rests.

3. Pour any excess fat from the skillet, then set it back over medium heat. Add the shallot, garlic, and rosemary; cook for 1 minute, or until fragrant, stirring frequently. Stir in the brandy. If the brandy ignites, cover the skillet and remove it from the heat for at least 30 seconds, or until the fire is out. Cook for 1 minute, or until the liquid in the pan is reduced by half and thickened. Swirl in the butter, if using, stirring until melted.

4. To serve, carve the meat away from the bone by running a chef's knife along the inside curve of the bone. Lay this "eye" of the meat on the carving board and slice it in half in the middle, as you would if you were slicing the layer of a cake open in the middle to frost it. Place one slice on each of two plates, then top with the shallot-rosemary sauce to serve. The bone is also quite delicious. Flip a coin to determine who gets it. Or devise your own reward system.

SAUTÉED VEAL CUTLETS *with* BUTTERY CARAWAY NOODLES

makes **2 hearty servings**

Veal cutlets make a quick dinner—as here, with a classic German preparation. You can also use this technique with thin pork cutlets, or with boneless, skinless chicken breasts, pounded thin. Follow this creamy entrée with a simple dessert such as strawberries, macerated in sugar, spiced with a little ground black pepper and a splash of aged balsamic vinegar.

Two 6-ounce veal cutlets
½ cup all-purpose flour
1 teaspoon mild paprika
1 teaspoon salt
½ teaspoon freshly ground black pepper
1 large egg, at room temperature
1 tablespoon milk (regular, low-fat, or nonfat)

½ cup plain dried bread crumbs
5 tablespoons unsalted butter
1½ teaspoons caraway seeds
6 ounces dried wide egg noodles, cooked according to the package instructions
1 tablespoon chopped fresh parsley, or 1 teaspoon dried parsley

1. Lay a sheet of plastic wrap on your work surface, place the cutlets on top of it, then cover with a second sheet of plastic wrap. Pound them to ¼-inch thickness with the smooth side of a meat mallet or the bottom of a heavy saucepan. Peel away both sheets of plastic wrap, slice each of the cutlets in half, and set the cutlets aside.

2. Mix the flour, paprika, salt, and pepper together on a large dinner plate. Lightly beat the egg with the milk in a wide, shallow bowl; set aside. Spread the bread crumbs onto a second large dinner plate.

3. Melt 3 tablespoons of the butter in a medium skillet set over medium-high heat. Working quickly, dredge the veal cutlets first in the flour mixture, shaking off any excess but making sure each is well coated. Dip them in the beaten egg mixture, then into the bread crumbs, coating both sides. Transfer the prepared cutlets to the skillet and fry for 4 minutes, or until golden brown on both sides, turning once. Transfer the cutlets to two dinner plates; tent with foil to keep warm.

4. Melt the remaining 2 tablespoons of butter in the skillet; as it melts, scrape up any browned bits stuck to the bottom of the skillet. Add the caraway seeds and toast for 15 seconds, stirring constantly. Add the cooked noodles and the parsley, toss well to coat, then cook for 30 seconds, or until heated through. Divide the noodles between the plates and serve at once.

Cookies

Is there anything better than cookies? But who wants to make six dozen when six will do? With these recipes, you don't have to stand over a hot oven bringing out tray after tray. One baking sheet, and you've got traditional sugar cookies or lemon hazelnut biscotti. Just one piece of advice: measure the ingredients precisely—there's a huge proportional difference between a 1 and 1½ teaspoons in these recipes. All in all, you'll have a batch of sweet indulgence, hot, moist, and ready to eat, without a cookie to spare.

CHOCOLATE CHIP
ESPRESSO COOKIES ⏱

makes **6 large cookies**

These chocolate chip cookies are spiked with instant espresso powder, available in most supermarkets alongside the other instant beverages, or with the teas and coffees. Look for *instant* espresso powder, a freeze-dried coffee, not just espresso powder (which is simply finely-ground espresso beans). The instant powder dissolves in the batter and gives the cookies a mild, mocha taste. Store instant espresso powder in the freezer, tightly sealed, for up to a year.

¼ cup packed light brown sugar

3 tablespoons unsalted butter, at room temperature

1 tablespoon pasteurized egg substitute, such as Egg Beaters; or 2 quail eggs

¼ teaspoon vanilla extract

7 tablespoons all-purpose flour

1 teaspoon instant espresso powder

¼ teaspoon baking soda

⅛ teaspoon salt

3 tablespoons semisweet or bittersweet chocolate chips, mini chocolate chips, or chocolate chunks, roughly chopped

1. Position the rack in the middle of the oven and preheat the oven to 350°F. Use a nonstick cookie sheet, or a regular one lined with either parchment paper or a silicon baking sheet.

2. Cream the brown sugar and butter in a small bowl with a wooden spoon or an electric mixer at low speed, until pale brown and fluffy, about 2 minutes by hand or 3 minutes with the mixer (see Note). Beat in the pasteurized egg substitute or the quail eggs and the vanilla for about 1 additional minute, until creamy. Using a wooden spoon, mix in the flour, espresso powder, baking soda, and salt all at once but just until incorporated; then gently stir in the chocolate chips. Do not use an electric mixer at this stage or the cookies will be tough.

3. Drop by six heaping tablespoonfuls onto the baking sheet. Gently press the cookies with the back of a stainless steel tablespoon, just until they flatten slightly—but do not press hard enough to turn them into disks. Bake for 10 minutes, or until brown and set. Transfer from the baking sheet to a wire rack and cool. Store them in a sealed container at room temperature for up to 2 days.

> NOTE: If the butter is very soft, the dough can easily be beaten with a wooden spoon. First, use the back of the spoon to mash the sugar into the butter, then turn the spoon around and begin beating the mixture until light and fluffy. This method produces dense cookies, since the batter is not whipped with air, as it is with a mixer. In any event, do not use a whisk— too much batter adheres to its wire whips, and small amounts of batter are precious when you're baking in small batches.

Hold the Espresso, Please.
For a small batch of standard chocolate chip cookies, without the mocha taste, simply omit the instant espresso powder from the recipe.

Peanut Butter Oatmeal Cookies

makes **6 cookies**

If you prefer a softer version of these classic cookies, take them out of the oven a minute or two earlier than suggested, just after they've set.

2 tablespoons packed light
  brown sugar
2 tablespoons granulated sugar
1½ tablespoons unsalted
  butter, at room
  temperature
1 tablespoon smooth peanut
  butter
1 tablespoon pasteurized
  egg substitute, such as Egg
  Beaters; or 2 quail eggs

⅛ teaspoon vanilla extract
3 tablespoons all-purpose flour
⅛ teaspoon baking soda
⅛ teaspoon ground cinnamon
⅛ teaspoon salt
6 tablespoons rolled oats (do
  not use quick-cooking oats)

1. Position the rack in the center of the oven and preheat the oven to 350°F. Use a nonstick cookie sheet, or a regular one lined with either parchment paper or a silicon baking sheet.

2. Cream the brown sugar, granulated sugar, and butter in a small bowl, using either a wooden spoon or an electric mixer at low speed, until the mixture is pale brown and smooth, about 2 minutes by hand or 1 minute with a mixer. Then beat in the peanut butter, the pasteurized egg substitute or the 2 quail eggs, and the vanilla until creamy, about 1 additional minute. With a wooden spoon, mix in the flour, baking soda, cinnamon, and salt all at once but just until moistened; then stir in the oats. Do not use an electric mixer at this stage or the dough will be overmixed.

3. Drop six heaping teaspoons of the dough on the cookie sheet, spacing the cookies about 2 inches apart. Bake for 12 minutes, or until set in the middle and lightly browned. Transfer the cookies to a wire rack to cool. Store them in a sealed container at room temperature for up to 2 days.

SUGAR COOKIES

makes **10 cookies**

To give the cookies a festive look, substitute 1 tablespoon colored sugar for the plain sugar you roll them in. If you prefer a softer cookie, take them out of the oven 1 to 2 minutes before suggested, just after they've set but are still soft in the center.

3 tablespoons solid vegetable shortening, plus additional for greasing the cookie sheet	¼ teaspoon vanilla extract
	½ cup all-purpose flour
6 tablespoons sugar	¼ teaspoon baking soda
1 medium egg yolk, at room temperature, or 2½ tablespoons pasteurized egg substitute, such as Egg Beaters; or 4 quail eggs	⅛ teaspoon cream of tartar
	⅛ teaspoon salt

1. Position a rack in the middle of the oven and preheat the oven to 400°F. Grease a cookie sheet with shortening. Place 1 tablespoon sugar in a small, shallow bowl and set aside.

2. Cream the 3 tablespoons shortening and the remaining 5 tablespoons of sugar in a medium bowl with an electric mixer at medium speed for about 3 minutes, or until light and fluffy. Beat in the egg and vanilla until creamy and smooth, about 30 seconds. Using a wooden spoon, stir in the flour, baking soda, cream of tartar, and salt, just until combined.

3. Roll a scant tablespoonful of the dough into a small ball between your palms. Roll this ball in the reserved sugar, then place on the prepared cookie sheet. Repeat with the remaining dough, making about ten sugar-covered balls; space them 2 inches apart on the cookie sheet. Gently flatten the balls with the back of the tines of a fork, going first in one direction, then rotating the fork 90 degrees for a second press, thereby making a crosshatch pattern in the cookie. Do not press the cookies flat, causing them to break at the edges.

4. Bake for 12 minutes, or just until firm. Transfer to a wire rack to cool. Store the cookies in a sealed container at room temperature for up to 3 days.

Cooking for Two

GINGERBREAD COOKIES

makes **8 large cookies**

These sweet molasses cookies taste just like gingerbread. They're also a little chewy, in keeping with the texture of gingerbread. Don't overbake them or the molasses will turn bitter. The cookies store well, up to 4 days tightly covered at room temperature. They're just the thing with a cup of tea.

3 tablespoons packed dark brown sugar

2 tablespoons plus 1 teaspoon unsalted butter, at room temperature

3 tablespoons unsulphured molasses

1 tablespoon pasteurized egg substitute, such as Egg Beaters; or 2 quail eggs

¼ teaspoon vanilla extract

¾ cup all-purpose flour, plus additional for dusting the work surface, a rolling pin, and your hands

1 teaspoon ground ginger

½ teaspoon baking soda

¼ teaspoon cream of tartar

⅛ teaspoon salt

1. Position the rack in the middle of the oven and preheat the oven to 350°F. Use a nonstick cookie sheet, or a regular one lined with either parchment paper or a silicon baking sheet.

2. Cream the brown sugar and butter in a small bowl with a wooden spoon or an electric mixer at low speed until the mixture is pale brown and fluffy, about 4 minutes by hand or 2 minutes with an electric mixer. Beat in the molasses, pasteurized egg substitute or quail eggs, and the vanilla for about 30 seconds, or until creamy. Using a wooden spoon, stir in the flour, ginger, baking soda, cream of tartar, and salt, all at once but just until incorporated.

3. Dust a clean, dry work surface with flour. Turn the sticky dough out onto the floured surface. Dust your hands with flour, then press the dough into a small disk with your palm. Dust this disk with flour. Dust the rolling pin with flour, then roll the dough disk into a circle about 11 inches in diameter and ¼ inch thick. Using a 3-inch round cookie cutter or a drinking glass, cut the dough into circles. Using a large metal spatula, transfer these to the baking sheet, spacing the cookies about 1 inch apart.

4. Bake for 12 minutes, or until set but soft, yet brown around the edges. Allow to stand on the cookie sheet at room temperature for 3 minutes, then transfer them to a wire rack to cool.

Cooking for Two

LINZER COOKIES

makes **2 large cookies**

Linzertorte is an Austrian specialty: a crunchy, almond crust, spread with jam, and topped with a lattice crust. Here, two wafer cookies sandwich raspberry jam—or any jam you prefer. They're perfect after any meal, or with a cup of tea midafternoon. Because the dough must be very fluffy and light, mix it only with an electric mixer, not by hand.

3 tablespoons solid vegetable shortening
3 tablespoons sugar
6 tablespoons slivered almonds, finely ground (see Note)
⅛ teaspoon finely grated lemon zest
½ cup all-purpose flour, plus additional for dusting the work surface and rolling pin

⅛ teaspoon baking powder
⅛ teaspoon ground cinnamon
⅛ teaspoon salt
1 tablespoon pasteurized egg substitute, such as Egg Beaters; or 2 quail eggs
3 tablespoons raspberry jam, or other jam
2 teaspoons confectioners' sugar

1. Position the rack in the bottom third of the oven and preheat the oven to 325°F. Use a nonstick cookie sheet, or a regular one lined with parchment paper, or a silicon baking sheet.

2. Cream the shortening and sugar in a medium bowl with an electric mixer at medium speed; continue beating for about 2 minutes, or until the mixture is light and fluffy, scraping down the sides of the bowl as necessary. Beat in the ground almonds and lemon zest until well incorporated; then beat in the flour, baking powder, cinnamon, and salt all at once. Finally, beat in the pasteurized egg substitute or the quail eggs, just until a dough forms. Alternatively, the dough can be made in a food processor; add the ingredients in the order listed above; pulse with each addition and scrape down the bowl as necessary.

3. Dust a clean, dry work surface with flour. Turn the dough out onto the floured surface, then press into a disk with the palm of your hand. Dust the dough and a rolling pin with flour; roll the dough to a ¼-inch-thick rectangle. With a sharp knife, cut out four 5½-inch-diameter circles. You can use a small tart pan, ramekin, or baking dish as your guide. Cut a round hole in the middle of two of these circles, about 2 inches wide. Use a wide spatula to transfer the four circles to the cookie sheet, spacing them about 1 inch apart.

4. Bake for 12 minutes, or until set and lightly browned. Cool the cookies for 5 minutes on the baking sheet, then transfer them to a wire rack to cool completely.

5. Spread 1½ tablespoons of raspberry jam on each of the two cookies without holes cut into them. Top these with the cookies with the holes cut out in the center. Dust each cookie with 1 teaspoon confectioners' sugar. Serve immediately; or store, covered, at room temperature for up to 2 days.

> **NOTE:** Grind almonds in a clean spice mill or a coffee grinder, in a mini food processor, or in a mortar with a pestle until the almonds resemble fine meal. You can also buy ground almonds in bulk at some health food stores.

LEMON HAZELNUT BISCOTTI

makes **8 biscotti**

Biscotti are twice-baked Italian cookies. They're dry and crisp, traditionally dunked into vin santo, red wine, or espresso. Cornmeal, a surprise ingredient here, makes these lemony biscotti very crunchy. Since one egg and a tiny amount of vanilla are the only liquids in this recipe, take extra care to measure the dry ingredients accurately.

¼ cup hazelnuts

1 large egg, lightly beaten, at room temperature; 3 tablespoons pasteurized egg substitute such as Egg Beaters, or 6 quail eggs

1 teaspoon vanilla extract

½ cup plus 1 tablespoon all-purpose flour, plus additional for dusting the work surface

5 tablespoons plus 1 teaspoon sugar

1 tablespoon plus 1 teaspoon cornmeal

½ teaspoon baking powder

⅛ teaspoon salt

2 tablespoons dried currants, or 2 tablespoons chopped black raisins

½ teaspoon grated lemon zest

¼ teaspoon ground ginger

1. Position the rack in the center of the oven and preheat the oven to 350°F. Place the hazelnuts on a lipped baking sheet (lipped so they won't roll off); bake for 7 minutes, or until fragrant and lightly browned, stirring once or twice. Maintain the oven's temperature, but cool the nuts for 5 minutes on the baking sheet, then pour them into a clean hand towel. Fold them into the towel and rub off their papery skins by rolling them between your hands inside the towel. Roughly chop the nuts with a heavy knife or in a mini food processor. Set them aside.

2. Lightly beat the egg, egg substitute, or quail eggs and vanilla in a small bowl with a fork; set aside. For baking the cookies, use a nonstick cookie sheet, or a regular one lined with either parchment paper or a silicon baking sheet.

Cookies

3. Stir the flour, sugar, cornmeal, baking powder, and salt in a medium bowl with a wooden spoon until well combined. Mix in the currants, lemon zest, ginger, and the chopped nuts; stir in the beaten egg. Continue stirring, although the dough will be quite dry, until the egg is thoroughly incorporated. Wash your hands and dry them thoroughly, then mix the dough by hand, kneading it in the bowl until it holds together. If the dough does not cohere (most likely because of the day's humidity or the viscosity of your flour's glutens), add water in 1-teaspoon increments, mixing by hand after each addition until it forms a compact but slightly dry dough.

4. Dust a clean, dry work surface with a small amount of flour. Turn the dough onto it, sprinkle lightly with flour, then roll the dough with your palms into a 6-inch-long log, about 2 inches in diameter, pressing down gently against the work surface as you form the log so that you get rid of any air pockets in the dough.

5. Place this log on the cookie sheet and bake for 35 minutes, until slightly cracked but barely browned. Cool on the cookie sheet for 5 minutes, then transfer the log to a wire rack to cool for 20 minutes. Meanwhile, reduce the oven temperature to 300°F.

6. Using a serrated knife, cut off the ends of the log, discard them, then slice the remaining log into 8 cookies. If you wish, make diagonal cuts across the log, so as to make larger cookies.

7. Return these cookies to the cookie sheet and bake for 25 minutes, turning once after 15 minutes. Transfer to a wire rack and cool completely. The cookies can be stored in a sealed container at room temperature for up to 5 days.

Cooking for Two

CHEWY
CHOCOLATE
ALMOND WAFERS

makes **8 cookies**

Thanks to the melted chocolate, these wafers have the fudgy consistency of fallen chocolate meringues. For best results, use a good-quality chocolate, not one larded with hydrogenated fat. Remove the cookies from the oven when they're still soft, then cool them completely before you enjoy them.

Unsalted butter for greasing the baking sheet
2 tablespoons sliced blanched almonds
⅓ cup packed dark brown sugar
2 tablespoons pasteurized egg substitute, such as Egg Beaters; or 4 quail eggs

½ ounce unsweetened chocolate, chopped, then melted and cooled slightly (to melt chocolate, see page 17)
¼ teaspoon vanilla extract
¼ cup all-purpose flour
¼ teaspoon baking soda
⅛ teaspoon salt

1. Position the rack in the middle of the oven and preheat the oven to 350°F. Butter a large cookie sheet; set aside. On a second baking sheet, toast the almonds in the oven for about 4 minutes, or until golden brown, stirring occasionally. Remove the almonds from the baking sheet and roughly chop them in a mini food processor, in a mortar and pestle, or on a cutting board with the knife. Set them aside.

2. Beat the brown sugar and pasteurized egg substitute or the quail eggs in a small bowl with an electric mixer at low speed until the mixture is pale brown, about 3 minutes. Slowly pour in the melted chocolate, beating all the while and scraping down the sides of the bowl with a rubber spatula. Beat in the vanilla until smooth.

3. Using a wooden spoon, stir in the flour, baking soda, and salt, just until moistened. Do not use an electric mixer or the batter will be over-mixed. Stir in the chopped toasted almonds, just until incorporated.

4. Drop the batter by heaping teaspoonfuls onto the prepared baking sheet, spacing the cookies about 2 inches apart. Bake for 10 minutes, until soft but nonetheless set. Cool on the baking sheet for 5 minutes, then transfer the cookies to a wire rack and cool completely. Store them in a sealed container at room temperature for up to 2 days.

WALNUT CHOCOLATE CHIP MERINGUE COOKIES 🍷🍷

makes **8 cookies**

These flourless cookies are actually made from marshmallowy seven-minute frosting that hasn't been beaten long enough to set up. Since they're baked for a long time at a low temperature, and even dried out in the oven once it's turned off, these are chewier than standard meringue cookies, although they still have that hard outer shell, which makes them perfect for dunking. Grind the walnuts in a mini food processor or in a mortar with a pestle.

1 large egg white, at room
    temperature
⅓ cup sugar
¼ teaspoon vanilla extract
⅛ teaspoon cream of tartar
⅛ teaspoon white wine vinegar,
    or white distilled vinegar
⅛ teaspoon salt

¼ cup walnut pieces, finely
    ground
2 tablespoons semisweet
    chocolate chips,
    mini chocolate chips,
    or chocolate chunks,
    roughly chopped

1. Position the rack in the bottom third of the oven and preheat the oven to 250°F. Use a nonstick cookie sheet, or a regular one lined with either parchment paper or a silicon baking sheet.

2. Bring 2 inches of water to a boil in the bottom of a double boiler or in a medium saucepan set over medium-high heat. Meanwhile, using an electric mixer at medium speed, beat the egg white, sugar, vanilla, cream of tartar, vinegar, and salt until smooth in the top of a double boiler or in a medium bowl that will fit snugly over the top of the saucepan.

3. Place the top of the double boiler or the bowl with this mixture over the simmering water; continue beating for 2 minutes, until thick, smooth, and quite shiny. Remove the top of the double boiler or the bowl from the simmering water. (Be careful of any escaping steam.) Stir in the nuts, then let the mixture cool in the bowl for 5 minutes. Stir in the chocolate chips.

4. Drop the batter by heaping tablespoonfuls onto the prepared cookie sheet. The cookies should look like large chocolate "kisses"—you can use the back of a metal spoon to mound them up a bit toward a center peak, but do not press down or the meringue will lose its airiness.

5. Bake for 1 hour 15 minutes, or until quite firm. Turn off the oven, prop the oven door open, and allow the cookies to sit in the oven for 1 hour. Transfer to a wire rack to cool completely. They can be stored in a sealed container at room temperature for up to 3 days.

Vanilla Orange Icebox Cookies 🧳

makes 8 cookies

Very old-fashioned, icebox cookies are made from a dough that's first chilled as a log in the refrigerator, then sliced off for baking. These orange-spiked butter cookies are crisp, making them excellent for dunking into coffee or a glass of dessert wine, such as one by Inniskillin. While they're very easy to make, we've labeled the recipe a "moderate" effort because the dough must be chilled for at least one hour before it can be baked. Thus, the recipe doesn't provide instant gratification—unless you've made the dough in advance and are just slicing off cookies to bake as you need them.

2 tablespoons sugar

1½ tablespoons unsalted butter, at room temperature

2 teaspoons pasteurized egg substitute, such as Egg Beaters; or 1 quail egg

¼ teaspoon vanilla extract

½ teaspoon grated orange zest

¼ cup plus 1 tablespoon all-purpose flour, plus additional for dusting the work surface and your hands

⅛ teaspoon baking powder

⅛ teaspoon salt

1. Cream the sugar and butter in a medium bowl with a wooden spoon for about 4 minutes, or with an electric mixer at medium speed for about 2 minutes, until fluffy and pale yellow. Beat in the pasteurized egg substitute or the quail egg, the vanilla, and the orange zest until smooth. Using a wooden spoon, stir in the flour, baking powder, and salt, just until incorporated. Do not use an electric mixer or the cookies will be overmixed and tough.

2. Dust a clean, dry work surface with flour. Turn the dough onto the work surface, dust your hands with flour, then roll the dough between your palms and the work surface into a small log, about 2¾ inches long and 1½ inches in diameter. Wrap the dough in plastic wrap and place it in the refrigerator to firm up, for at least 1 hour or up to 5 days.

3. Position the rack in the middle of the oven and preheat the oven to 350°F. Use a nonstick cookie sheet, or a regular one lined with either parchment paper or a silicon baking sheet. Unwrap the dough and cut it into ¼-inch-thick slices. (Cut off the ends for perfect cookies.) Place the cookies on the cookie sheet at least 1 inch apart. Bake for 10 minutes, or until firm. Cool for 2 minutes on the cookie sheet, then transfer to a wire rack to cool completely. The cookies can be stored in a sealed container at room temperature for up to 3 days.

ONE COOKIE AT A TIME

Of course, icebox cookies are the ultimate small-batch treat—you can make the dough log in advance, store it in your refrigerator, and make as many cookies as you want at any time, from one to eight.

CHOCOLATE CHILE ICEBOX COOKIES

makes **8 cookies**

These cookies are made with chocolate and cayenne pepper, an inspired combination for sweets, traditional in many Texas bakeries. The dense, chocolate cookies are not hot, just slightly spicy. If you're not so adventurous, omit the cayenne for traditional chocolate icebox cookies. As with the Vanilla Orange Icebox Cookies, you can make the dough log ahead.

4½ tablespoons all-purpose flour, plus additional for dusting the work surface and your hands

2 tablespoons plus 1 teaspoon cocoa powder, preferably not Dutch-processed

½ teaspoon cayenne pepper

4½ tablespoons unsalted butter, at room temperature

3 tablespoons sugar

2½ teaspoons pasteurized egg substitute, such as Egg Beaters; or 1 quail egg

¼ teaspoon vanilla extract

1. Sift the flour, cocoa powder, and cayenne together; set aside.

2. Cream the butter and sugar in a medium bowl with a wooden spoon or an electric mixer at low speed, until fluffy and light, about 5 minutes by hand or 3 minutes with a mixer. Beat in the pasteurized egg substitute or the quail egg and the vanilla until smooth. Using a wooden spoon, stir in the reserved flour mixture just until combined.

3. Dust a clean, dry work surface with flour; turn the dough out onto it. Dust your hands with flour and roll the very soft dough between your palms and the work surface into a log about 1½ inches in diameter and 2½ inches long. Wrap this log tightly in plastic wrap; then refrigerate until firm, for at least 1 hour or up to 5 days.

4. To bake the cookies, position the rack in the center of the oven and preheat the oven to 375°F. Use a nonstick cookie sheet, or a regular one lined with either parchment paper or a silicon baking sheet. Cut the chilled log into ¼-inch-thick slices. (For perfect cookies, discard the rough, rounded ends.) Space the cookies 2 inches apart on the cookie sheet. Bake for 10 minutes, or just until set. Cool on the cookie sheet for 5 minutes, then transfer to a wire rack to cool completely. Store them in a sealed container at room temperature for up to 3 days.

Puddings

Pudding for two? It might not seem practical, or even possible—but truth is, you can make a custard in a small batch just as easily as in a large one. You'll need some small bowls or ramekins, and some accurate measuring tools for minuscule amounts of ingredients; but in no time, you can have an old-fashioned vanilla pudding or a luscious crème brûlée.

VANILLA PUDDING ⏱

makes 2 small bowls of pudding

We're partial to the basics—so what could be better than vanilla pudding? To assure the creamiest pudding, strain it before you put it in the bowls, to make sure you remove any bits of cooked egg or unincorporated flour.

2 large egg yolks, at room temperature (to save the egg whites, see page 9); or 4 quail eggs
1 cup milk (regular, low-fat, or nonfat)

2 tablespoons all-purpose flour
¼ cup sugar
⅛ teaspoon salt
1 teaspoon vanilla extract

1. Whisk the egg yolks or whole quail eggs in a small bowl until smooth and uniform; set aside.

2. Whisk the milk, flour, sugar, and salt in a medium saucepan set over medium heat until the flour is incorporated, the sugar has dissolved, and the mixture thickens and comes to a simmer. Continue to cook at a simmer, whisking constantly, for 30 seconds.

3. Remove the pan from the heat and slowly whisk ½ cup of the milk mixture into the beaten egg yolks. Whisk this egg yolk mixture back into the pan with the remainder of the pudding. Reduce the heat to very low. Set the pan over the heat, whisk in the vanilla, and cook for just 20 seconds to set the egg yolks, whisking constantly to keep the mixture from scorching. Make sure you reach into the corners of the pan with the whisk.

4. Strain the pudding through a fine-mesh sieve into two 1-cup ramekins or bowls, or a medium serving bowl. Place in the refrigerator for about 2 hours to cool and set (see Note). You can make this pudding up to 3 days ahead of time; cover with plastic wrap and store in the refrigerator.

NOTE: Some people love the skin that forms on pudding as it sets; others are not as enthralled. To keep the pudding from forming a skin, lay a piece of plastic wrap directly on the exposed surface of the pudding while it is still warm; seal the bowl with the plastic wrap and then refrigerate. To serve, gently pull off the plastic wrap, which will have inhibited the formation of that infamous skin.

Variations

Whisk any of the following into the custard with the vanilla:

2 crumbled Oreos or gingersnap cookies
2 tablespoons currants or chopped raisins or chopped dried cranberries
2 tablespoons chopped candied (or glacéed) fruit
½ teaspoon ground cinnamon
¼ teaspoon grated nutmeg

CINNAMON ALMOND
CHOCOLATE PUDDING

makes 2 small bowls of pudding

This pudding was inspired by Mexican chocolate—that is, chocolate blended with cinnamon, vanilla, and ground almonds or cocoa nibs. Unfortunately, the chocolate in Mexican chocolate isn't always of the highest grade. If you start with good-quality chocolate, you'll have those traditional flavors in this pudding, but with a more luxurious texture and taste.

1 large egg yolk, at room temperature (to save the egg white, see page 9); or 2 whole quail eggs	¼ cup sugar
	¼ cup packed light brown sugar
	1 tablespoon all-purpose flour
1 cup milk (regular, low-fat, or nonfat)	⅛ teaspoon ground cinnamon
	½ teaspoon vanilla extract
1 ounce unsweetened chocolate, finely chopped	⅛ teaspoon almond extract

1. Lightly beat the egg yolk or quail eggs with a fork in a small bowl; set aside.

2. Mix the milk, chocolate, sugar, brown sugar, flour, and cinnamon in a small pan. Set the pan over very low heat and whisk until the chocolate melts and the mixture is smooth. Raise the heat to medium and continue whisking until the mixture begins to simmer. Reduce the heat to very low and simmer for 1 minute, whisking constantly.

3. Whisk 2 tablespoons of this hot chocolate mixture into the egg yolk, then whisk the chocolate-egg yolk mixture back into the pan. Return the pan to low heat; continue cooking and whisking until the mixture thickens slightly, about 30 seconds. For a more accurate test of its doneness, dip a wooden spoon into the chocolate mixture, then run your finger across the back of the spoon. The line you make in the chocolate mixture should stay put, without any running.

4. Remove the pan from the heat, whisk in the vanilla and almond extracts, then pour this mixture into two 1-cup ramekins or bowls, or into one 2-cup serving bowl. Place in the refrigerator to cool and set, about 2 hours. (On the serious subject of pudding skin, see page 229.) You can make this pudding up to 2 days ahead of time; cover it with plastic wrap and store it in the refrigerator.

Baked Rice Pudding 🧳

makes 2 small ramekins of rice pudding

Rice pudding is one of those desserts that comes coated with all the nostalgia of a June Cleaver household. No wonder: it's comforting, creamy, and delicious. The custard rises to the top as it bakes, forming a creamy layer over the rice. Here, we've studded the custard with dried cranberries and spiked it with crystallized ginger—but you can omit both and double the vanilla for a more standard pudding.

½ cup plus 2 tablespoons water

¼ cup white rice (do not use instant rice)

Unsalted butter for greasing the ramekins

2 tablespoons sugar

2 tablespoons dried cranberries

1 tablespoon finely chopped crystallized ginger

1 large egg, plus 1 large egg yolk, at room temperature; or 1 large egg, plus 2 whole quail eggs

1¼ cups milk (regular, low-fat, or nonfat)

¼ teaspoon vanilla extract

⅛ teaspoon salt

1. Bring the water to a simmer in a small saucepan set over medium-high heat. Stir in the rice, cover, then reduce the heat to low. Cook for about 15 minutes, or until the rice is tender. Meanwhile, position the rack in the middle of the oven and preheat the oven to 350°F. Butter two 1½-cup oven-safe ramekins (about 3½ inches wide and 2 inches deep); set aside.

2. Transfer the warm rice to a medium bowl and stir in the sugar, cranberries, and crystallized ginger. In a separate small bowl, whisk the egg, egg yolk, milk, vanilla, and salt until uniform. Pour this mixture over the rice mixture and stir with a wooden spoon until well combined.

3. Divide the rice-and-milk mixture between the two prepared ramekins. Place these ramekins in a small roasting pan or a shallow casserole. Fill the roasting pan with hot water until it comes halfway up the sides of the ramekins. Bake in this water bath for 40 minutes, or until a knife comes out clean when inserted into the center of the custard. Serve warm, or let stand at room temperature until cooled, then cover with plastic wrap and store in the refrigerator for up to 2 days.

MAPLE CRÈME BRÛLÉE 💼

makes **2 crème brûlées**

Although crème brûlée inspires fervid devotees, it's really a simple dessert, a creamy custard with a burned sugar topping. Here, we've lightened the original somewhat, using half-and-half rather than cream (which you can, of course, use for the original decadence). For best results, use real maple syrup, preferably Grade A Dark Amber, a sturdier, heartier maple syrup, which is not as delicate as the Grade A Light Amber usually served with pancakes.

1 cup half-and-half
2 tablespoons maple syrup, preferably dark amber grade
2 large egg yolks, at room temperature; or 4 whole quail eggs

½ teaspoon cornstarch
½ teaspoon vanilla extract
4 teaspoons sugar, preferably superfine sugar

1. Position the rack in the center of the oven and preheat the oven to 350°F. Place the half-and-half in a small saucepan and warm it over low heat until small bubbles form around the sides of the pan. Meanwhile, beat the syrup and egg yolks or quail eggs in a medium bowl with a whisk until pale yellow, about 3 minutes.

2. Whisk the cornstarch into the yolk mixture, then whisk in about ¼ cup of the warmed half-and-half, drizzling it in a thin, steady stream. Continue whisking until the mixture is uniform, then whisk this egg yolk mixture back into the saucepan with the half-and-half. Cook over low heat for about 1 minute, or just until slightly thickened, whisking constantly. You can also test for doneness by dipping a wooden spoon into the hot mixture, then running your finger across the back of the spoon. The line you make should stay in place, without sagging or without cream running into it. Stir in the vanilla.

3. Pour the slightly thickened custard into two small, shallow, heat-safe baking dishes, ramekins, or custard cups, each about ¾ cup to 1 cup in size. Place these baking dishes in a medium roasting pan or a shallow casserole dish; add hot water to the roasting pan until the water comes halfway up the sides of the baking dishes. Bake in this water bath for 50 minutes. To test for doneness, jiggle the pan gently—the custard should appear set. Remove the baking dishes from the water bath, place them on a wire rack, and cool for 5 minutes. The dessert can be made in advance up to this point; cool the custard to room temperature, then cover and store in the refrigerator for up to 2 days. Let the custards return to room temperature before preparing the topping.

4. Sprinkle each custard with 2 teaspoons sugar. Burn the sugar on the top of each custard with a kitchen blowtorch. Alternatively, preheat the broiler and broil the custards on a broiler rack or baking sheet set about 4 to 6 inches from the heat source; broil until the sugar is caramelized, about 2 minutes. Cool for 5 minutes, then serve; or let stand at room temperature for up to 1 hour before serving.

Fruit
Desserts

Just a pear or two or a crisp apple—a little bit of fruit makes a great dessert for two, whether quite simple, as in Baked Bananas with Rum, or very elegant, such as Lemon Meringue Tartlets. There's only one rule of thumb for buying fresh fruit: if it doesn't smell like anything, it won't taste like anything either. So buy the best you can find and discover fruit desserts—for the first time or once again.

APPLE CRANBERRY COBBLER

makes **2 servings**

This cobbler filling is thickened with tapioca, which gives the apples and cranberries the rich taste and texture of a pie filling. The crackly topping includes cornmeal for good crunch. Serve with scoops of vanilla ice cream, dollops of sweetened whipped cream, or sweetened crème fraîche.

3 tablespoons plus 1 teaspoon unsalted butter, melted	1½ teaspoons quick-cooking tapioca
2 tablespoons chopped pecans	1 teaspoon orange zest
1 quart water	¼ teaspoon salt
2 cups whole cranberries	¼ cup all-purpose flour
1 medium tart apple (about 6 ounces), such as a Granny Smith, peeled, cored, and thinly sliced	2 tablespoons rolled oats (do not use quick-cooking oats)
	2 tablespoons cornmeal
¾ cup sugar	½ teaspoon vanilla extract
	⅛ teaspoon ground cinnamon

1. Position the rack in the middle of the oven and preheat the oven to 350°F. Butter a shallow 2½-cup au gratin dish or any shallow 2½-cup baking dish; set aside. Toast the pecans in a small, dry skillet set over medium-low heat for about 3 minutes, or until they are lightly browned and fragrant, stirring often; set aside.

2. Bring the water to a boil in a medium saucepan set over high heat. Add the cranberries and cook for about 2 minutes, or until half of them pop. Drain, then transfer them to a medium bowl. Stir in the apple slices, ½ cup of the sugar, the tapioca, orange zest, the 1 teaspoon melted butter, and ⅛ teaspoon of the salt. Pour this mixture into the prepared baking dish; set aside while you prepare the topping.

3. In a clean medium bowl, mix the remaining 3 tablespoons of the melted butter with the flour, oats, cornmeal, pecans, vanilla, cinnamon, and the remaining ⅛ teaspoon of the salt, just until moistened. Gently spread this mixture over the apple filling without pushing down. Wetting the back of a metal teaspoon can help spread the crust without its sticking; or use your fingers to crumble the topping over the fruit filling, distributing it evenly across the surface.

4. Bake for 35 minutes, or until the filling is bubbling and the topping is set like a crust. Let stand for 5 minutes before serving.

Cranberries

Buy fresh cranberries in clear bags, so you can see what you're getting. The berries should be bright red or maroon; discard any that are soft or mushy. Cranberries freeze exceptionally well; toss the bags into the freezer, where the berries will keep for a year. Once frozen, they are best used in pies and cobblers, since they will break down when defrosted.

RUSTIC APPLE TART 💼

makes **one 6-inch tart**

A rustic tart is a free-form pie. The crust is laid on a baking sheet and the edges are simply folded over the filling. Use very cold water to make the crust—it will keep the shortening from liquefying into the flour until it's baked. A little bit of vinegar gives the crust a crisp, cookie-like crunch.

½ cup all-purpose flour, plus additional for dusting the work surface and rolling pin

2 tablespoons plus 1 teaspoon sugar

3 tablespoons solid vegetable shortening

2 tablespoons ice water

¼ teaspoon apple cider vinegar

2 small apples (about 5 ounces each), peeled, cored, and thinly sliced (see Note)

¼ teaspoon ground cinnamon

Pinch of salt

1. Position the rack in the bottom third of the oven and preheat the oven to 375°F. Mix the flour and 1 tablespoon of the sugar in a medium bowl. Cut in the shortening with a pastry cutter or two forks, until the mixture resembles coarse meal; stir in the ice water and vinegar with a fork, just until a dough forms.

2. Dust a clean, dry work surface with flour, turn the dough out onto it, and press lightly into a small disk. Dust the disk and a rolling pin with flour. Roll the dough into an 8-inch circle, then transfer to a lipped baking sheet, preferably nonstick or one lined with either parchment paper or a silicon baking sheet. Use a wide spatula to transfer the dough; or gently fold it in half to help transport it to the baking sheet, but do not crease it.

3. Spread the apple slices in the middle of the dough circle, mounding them slightly toward the middle and leaving a 1-inch border around the dough's edges. Sprinkle the remaining 1 tablespoon plus 1 teaspoon of sugar over the apples, as well as the cinnamon and the salt.

4. Gently fold the edges of the dough over the filling, creating a loose, buckling top over the apples but leaving the center hole open.

5. Bake for 45 minutes, or until the crust is lightly browned and the filling is bubbling. Cool for 5 minutes on the baking sheet before serving.

> **NOTE:** Do not substitute one large apple. The individual slices will be too large for the small tart.

LEMON MERINGUE TARTLETS

makes **2 tarts**

For an elegant dessert, try these two little tarts, filled with a streamlined lemon curd, piled high with meringue, and baked until browned. To get the most height out of the meringue, remember these three rules of thumb: 1) the egg white must be at room temperature, 2) the beaters and mixing bowl should be at room temperature and completely dry, and 3) there cannot be one speck of yolk in the egg white.

FOR THE CRUST

½ cup all-purpose flour, plus additional for dusting the work surface and rolling pin

⅛ teaspoon salt

3 tablespoons solid vegetable shortening

1½ to 2 tablespoons ice water

FOR THE FILLING

1 large egg yolk, lightly beaten, at room temperature

6 tablespoons water

6 tablespoons sugar

2½ teaspoons cornstarch

1½ tablespoons lemon juice (the juice of 1 small lemon)

1 teaspoon grated lemon zest

FOR THE MERINGUE

1 large egg white, at room temperature

⅛ teaspoon salt, or less to taste

1½ tablespoons sugar

⅛ teaspoon vanilla extract

1. Position the rack in the bottom third of the oven and preheat the oven to 425°F.

2. To make the crust, mix the flour and salt in a small bowl. Cut in the shortening with a pastry cutter or two forks, until the mixture resembles coarse meal. Stir in the ice water with a fork, just until the mixture forms a dough. Dust a clean, dry work surface with flour, divide the dough into two equal balls, and place one on the work surface and the other under a clean kitchen towel to keep moist. Dust the first ball and a rolling pin with flour, then roll the dough into a 6-inch circle. Lay this circle in a 4½-inch tart pan with a removable bottom or a 4-inch paper pastry shell, lightly pressing the dough against the pan's sides and bottom. Prick with a fork, then line the crust with aluminum foil or parchment paper. Fill the lined tart shell with pie weights or dry beans. If you use dry beans, they will no longer be fit to eat—but you can reuse them to weight other tart shells and pie crusts. Repeat with the second dough ball and a second tart pan or shell.

3. Bake for 15 minutes. Remove the pie weights or beans, and bake for another 5 minutes, or until beige and flaky. Transfer the pie shells to a wire rack and cool. The recipe can be made ahead to this point. When they are completely cooled, seal the tart shells in plastic wrap and store at room temperature for up to 2 days.

4. To make the filling, lightly beat the egg yolk in a small bowl; set aside. Whisk the water, sugar, and cornstarch in a small saucepan. Set the pan over medium heat and whisk constantly until the sugar dissolves, then stir in the lemon juice and lemon zest. Bring the mixture to a simmer, whisking constantly. Reduce the heat to low and continue simmering for 3 minutes, or until thickened, whisking constantly.

5. Whisk ¼ cup of the hot lemon mixture into the egg yolk until smooth, then whisk this lemon mixture back into the saucepan. Return the saucepan to very low heat and continue cooking and whisking for about 15 seconds, just to set the eggs. Do not let the mixture return to a boil. Divide this hot mixture between the two prepared tart shells and set them aside to cool for 15 minutes on a wire rack.

6. To make the meringue, increase the oven temperature to 500°F. Beat the egg white and salt in a small bowl with an electric mixer at medium speed until foamy. Slowly add the sugar in a steady, needle-thin stream, beating all the while; continue beating until soft peaks form, scraping down the sides of the bowl with a clean, dry rubber spatula as necessary. Do not overbeat—the peaks should be glistening and moist (see Note).

Quickly beat in the vanilla, just until combined. Spoon the beaten egg white mixture onto each of the two filled tart shells, gently spreading it to the edges with the back of a teaspoon. Do not press down, or you will lose some of the rise in the meringue. Seal the edges by gently pushing the meringue against the crust until it adheres all the way around and there are no gaps.

7. Bake for about 4 minutes, or until the meringue is lightly browned. Cool for at least 10 minutes before serving. If you've used a tart pan with a removable bottom, tap the bottom of the pie shells to loosen their edges. Push the bottom of the tart shell up until the tart comes clean of the metal sides. Once the tart is free of the form's metal sides, run a thin knife under the removable bottoms to loosen the tarts from the metal bottom, then gently transfer the tarts to two serving plates. If you've used a paper pastry shell, either peel it away from the tart or simply serve the tart in its paper shell, scooping it out to eat it.

> **NOTE:** To test if egg whites are properly beaten, turn off the mixer and lift the still beaters out of the egg whites; silky, droopy, but somewhat firm peaks should form where the beaters have pulled the mixture up. You may need to dip the still beaters into the mixture once or twice to tell. If you rub a pinch of meringue between your fingers, you should feel no sugar granules.

STRAWBERRY
CHOCOLATE TARTLETS 🍷🍷

makes **2 tarts**

These are old-fashioned strawberry tarts. They're topped with whipped cream and have a vanilla-wafer crust, which is spread with melted chocolate as a base for the strawberries.

FOR THE CRUST
16 vanilla wafer cookies
2 teaspoons sugar
2 tablespoons unsalted butter,
    melted and cooled

FOR THE FILLING
1 pint ripe strawberries
¼ cup sugar, preferably
    superfine sugar

⅓ cup semisweet or
    bittersweet chocolate
    chips, 2 tablespoons melted
    (see page 17), the
    remainder reserved
    separately
1 cup heavy cream
1 tablespoon amaretto,
    hazelnut liqueur, or other
    nut liqueur

1. Position the rack in the middle of the oven and preheat the oven to 375°F. To make the crust, grind the vanilla wafers and sugar in a food processor, a mini food processor, or a blender. Pour this mixture into a small bowl and stir in the melted butter, until thoroughly moistened. Press half this cookie mixture into each of two 4½-inch tart pans with removable bottoms, or two 4-inch paper pastry shells. Place the crust on a lipped baking sheet.

2. Bake the crusts for 10 minutes. When they come out of the oven, use a teaspoon to press down any parts that have puffed up. Set the tart shells on a wire rack to cool completely. The recipe can be made in advance up to this point; store the tart shells, tightly covered, at room temperature for up to 2 days.

3. To make the filling, slice the strawberries and place them in a small bowl. Stir in 1 tablespoon of the sugar; set aside to macerate for 30 minutes.

4. Meanwhile, brush half of the melted chocolate into the bottom of each of the two cooled tart shells; set aside to cool and harden for 10 minutes. If using tart pans with removable bottoms, remove the sides from the tart by pushing up gently from the bottom, taking care not to break the crusts. Slip off the metal bottoms by running a thin knife between the crust and bottom. If using paper pastry shells, leave them on the crust because tearing them away can pull off too much of this delicate cookie shell. Place the tart shells onto two serving plates.

5. Divide the strawberries and any accumulated juice between the two chocolate-coated tart shells.

6. Beat the whipped cream in a small bowl with an electric mixer at medium speed until foamy. Gradually add in the remaining 3 table-spoons sugar, beating constantly, just until the sugar has dissolved and soft peaks form, but not until the whipped cream becomes dry and but-tery (see Note). Alternatively, place the cream and sugar in a mini food processor and pulse until a light whipped cream forms. Stir in the remaining chocolate chips and the amaretto. Mound this mixture over the tarts, dividing it between the two filled shells and sealing it against the crust. Serve immediately, or set in the refrigerator to chill for up to 2 hours. If desired, wrap very loosely in plastic wrap to preserve the tarts from any refrigerator odors.

> **NOTE:** For the best peaks with whipped cream, make sure the bowl and the mixer's beaters are completely dry but well chilled.

BAKED BANANAS WITH RUM

makes **2 servings**

For this easy dessert, bananas are baked in a sauce of butter, rum, and jam. Serve with scoops of vanilla ice cream, vanilla frozen yogurt, sweetened whipped cream, or sweetened sour cream.

2 teaspoons unsalted butter, plus additional for greasing the aluminum foil	1 tablespoon plus 1 teaspoon apricot jam
2 large bananas, peeled, split lengthwise, then cut in half	1 tablespoon dark rum
	¼ teaspoon vanilla extract
	⅛ teaspoon ground cinnamon

1. Position the rack in the lower third of the oven and preheat the oven to 450°F. Butter a piece of aluminum foil large enough to cover a small 2½-cup au gratin dish or other 2½-cup shallow baking dish; set aside.

2. Place the bananas in the baking dish; dot with the butter and jam. Drizzle the rum and vanilla over the top, then sprinkle with ground cinnamon. Seal tightly with the prepared foil, buttered side down. Bake for 15 minutes, until bubbly. Serve warm, mounded in serving bowls.

Baked Fruit
Instead of the bananas, try sliced peaches or nectarines, halved pitted apricots or plums, or pineapple slices. All will bake up sweet and soft with the jam and butter. Increase the baking time to 20 minutes for the stone fruits, and to 25 minutes for the pineapple.

GINGER HONEY POACHED PEARS 🧳

makes 2 poached pears

Here, fresh pears are poached in an aromatic honey syrup. Buy firm Bosc pears with no soft spots, so the fruit will hold up while cooking. Serve this dessert with sweetened whipped cream—or make the pears the night before and enjoy them the next morning for breakfast.

1 cup water
½ cup plus 2 tablespoons
   sugar
One 4-inch piece of peeled
   fresh ginger, thinly sliced
2 Bosc pears with stems
   attached

1 tablespoon honey, preferably
   a very fragrant honey, such
   as pine, acacia, rosemary,
   or wildflower

1. Stir the water, ¼ cup plus 2 tablespoons of the sugar, and the ginger in a small pot or medium saucepan until the sugar dissolves. Place the pan over medium-high heat and bring the mixture to a simmer.

2. Meanwhile, cut about ¼ inch off the bottom of each of the pears, so they have a flat surface to stand on when served. Core the pears with a small melon baller. Scoop up from the bottom end into the flesh, turning the melon baller as you press in. It usually takes about two scoops to get out all the seeds. Alternatively, use a sharp knife to make an X in the bottom of each pear, then begin coring out this X with the knife, taking care not to slice deeply into the sides or remove too much of the flesh.

3. When the water is boiling, place the pears on their sides in the pot. If you place them oppositely front to back, they will fit more easily. Cover, reduce the heat to low, and simmer for 20 minutes, gently turning the pears in the syrup a couple of times. When done, the pears will be tender when pierced with a knife. Use a slotted spoon to remove them gently to a small bowl.

4. Strain the liquid in the pot, discarding the ginger but reserving ⅓ cup of the liquid. Return this to the pot, then stir in the remaining ¼ cup of sugar. Set the pot over medium-high heat and bring the mixture to a boil, stirring until the sugar dissolves. Once the sugar has dissolved and the mixture is boiling, cook for 3 minutes without stirring, until thickened. Remove the pot from the heat and stir in the honey as well as any liquid given off by the pears in the bowl. Stir until smooth, then pour this mixture over the pears. Cool to room temperature before serving. If desired, cover with plastic wrap and store in the refrigerator for up to 3 days. Serve chilled or at room temperature.

SPICED FRUIT COMPOTE

makes 2 generous servings

Spiced fruit compote: it's a dessert right out of grandmother's kitchen. Unfortunately, when we were kids, it often turned into raisin-and-prune sludge, made in cauldron-sized batches. Here, we've cut down the recipe and updated it with dried red plums, pears, and nectarines. It's sweet, perfumey, and very comforting on a cold winter night—or great for breakfast on a summer morning. The dried fruits used here are available in bulk at most gourmet markets and health food stores.

1¼ cup water	6 dried red plum halves,
½ cup sugar	roughly chopped
One 4-inch cinnamon stick	4 dried pear halves, roughly
4 whole cloves	chopped
2 cardamom pods	4 dried nectarine or peach
1 star anise pod	halves, roughly chopped

1. Whisk the water and sugar in a medium saucepan set over medium heat until the sugar dissolves, then add the cinnamon stick, cloves, cardamom pods, and anise pod. Bring the mixture to a simmer and add the dried plums, pears, and nectarines. Cover, reduce the heat to low, and simmer for 30 minutes, or until the dried fruit is quite soft.

2. Remove the pan from the heat, cover, and let stand at room temperature for 1 hour. Discard the spices. Serve at once; or store, covered, in the refrigerator for up to 3 days.

Serving Suggestions
Serve this compote in bowls with cookies on the side, if you wish, as well as

a dollop of sweetened whipped cream
a scoop of frozen vanilla yogurt
a scoop of vanilla ice cream
a small round of soft goat cheese
a spoonful of crème fraîche
a spoonful of plain yogurt

COCONUT CREPES WITH TROPICAL FRUIT SAUCE 🍷🍷

makes 6 small crepes

Although these lightly sweetened crepes are easy to make, they're quite chic, studded with coconut and served with a sauce of puréed kiwi and passion fruit. Baby pineapples are available in some markets; look for a fruit that is very aromatic without any soft spots. If you can't find one, substitute an 8-ounce can of pineapple chunks in juice (not syrup), drained.

FOR THE SAUCE
2 small kiwis, peeled
1 ripe baby pineapple, peeled, cored, and roughly chopped
1 ripe passion fruit (see Note)
1 tablespoon sugar
1 teaspoon lime juice

FOR THE CREPES
½ cup all-purpose flour
2 teaspoons sugar
⅛ teaspoon salt
One 5½-ounce can coconut milk

6 tablespoons milk (regular, low-fat, or nonfat)
1 large egg, lightly beaten, at room temperature, or 3 tablespoons pasteurized egg substitute such as Egg Beaters, or 6 quail eggs
2 tablespoons sweetened shredded coconut
1 teaspoon (or more) unsalted butter, at room temperature, for greasing the skillet

1. To make the sauce, purée the peeled kiwi fruit in a food processor, a mini food processor, or a wide-bottom blender. You may need to add 1 or 2 teaspoons water if you're using a blender. Pour this purée into a small bowl and mix with the chopped pineapple.

2. Cut the passion fruit open and scrape the seeds into the puréed kiwi fruit. Stir in the sugar and lime juice; continue stirring until the sugar dissolves. Set aside. The recipe can be made ahead of time up to this point. Store the sauce, covered, in the refrigerator for up to 2 days.

3. To make the crepes, combine the flour, sugar, and salt in a medium bowl; set aside. In a separate medium bowl, beat the coconut milk, milk, and egg, egg substitute, or quail eggs until frothy and uniform, using either a whisk or an electric mixer at medium speed. Then beat the coconut milk mixture into the prepared flour mixture, either by hand with a whisk or with the electric mixer; beat just until smooth, about 1 minute by hand or 30 seconds with an electric mixer. Stir in the shredded coconut.

4. Heat a 10-inch skillet, preferably nonstick, over medium heat. Add 1 teaspoon of the butter and swirl the skillet so the melted butter completely coats the bottom. Pour a scant ¼ cup batter into the skillet; shake the skillet vigorously so that the batter spreads out over the entire surface. Cook for 1 minute, just until set. Flip the crepe with a nonstick heat-safe spatula or a heat-safe rubber spatula, then cook for 1 more minute, or until lightly browned. Transfer the crepe to a serving plate and repeat with the remaining batter until 6 crepes are made, placing 3 on each plate. (You can keep them warm in a 250°F oven, if you wish.) You may need to add more butter to the pan, depending on how well seasoned it is, and how sticky the batter has gotten. Add butter in 1-teaspoon increments, swirling it around the pan to coat as necessary.

5. To serve, either spoon some of the sauce into a crepe and fold it closed over the sauce, or roll the coconut crepes into tubes and pour the sauce over them.

> **NOTE:** Passion fruit is ripe when it looks well beyond its prime: the skin should be wrinkled, shriveled, blackened, and quite soft.

Cakes *and* Other Treats

A cake for two? Why not? With small pans, you can turn out a couple of small cheesecakes or single-serving carrot cakes with even less trouble than required by their larger kin. A dab of icing or a scoop of ice cream—and you're done. Best of all, you can indulge tonight without staring at the cake on the counter for the rest of the week.

BROWNIES ⏱

Brownies may be the quintessential American treat. We should know, having written the ultimate book on them! But before the modern conveniences of larger ovens and baking pans, brownies were made in individual tins. So in some senses, we've returned them to their roots by making them in two small 1-cup ceramic ramekins. Don't use paper pastry shells or springform pans—they're too wide to be successful. The narrower ramekins make dense, fudgy brownies. (For outlets to buy ramekins, see the Source Guide, page 269.)

1 tablespoon plus 1 teaspoon unsalted butter, melted and cooled, plus additional for greasing the ramekins

1 tablespoon plus 1 teaspoon all-purpose flour, plus additional for dusting the ramekins

½ ounce unsweetened chocolate, chopped, melted, and cooled slightly (see page 17)

3 tablespoons packed light brown sugar

1 tablespoon pasteurized egg substitute, such as Egg Beaters; or 2 quail eggs

¼ teaspoon vanilla extract

⅛ teaspoon baking powder

⅛ teaspoon salt

1. Position the rack in the center of the oven and preheat the oven to 350°F. Butter and flour two 1-cup ramekins; set them aside. Mix the melted butter and melted chocolate together in a small bowl until smooth, using a wooden spoon or a whisk; set aside.

2. Beat the brown sugar, pasteurized egg substitute or quail eggs, and vanilla in a medium bowl until fluffy and pale brown, about 3 minutes with a whisk or 2 minutes with an electric mixer at medium speed. Beat in the melted chocolate mixture; continue beating until smooth. Using a wooden spoon, stir in the 1 tablespoon plus 1 teaspoon flour, the baking powder, and salt, just until combined. Do not beat with an electric mixer at this stage. Divide this mixture between the two prepared ramekins.

3. Bake for about 22 minutes, or until a cake tester or toothpick comes out with a few moist crumbs attached. Cool on a wire rack in the ramekins, then unmold to serve. When completely cooled, the brownies can be wrapped in plastic wrap and stored at room temperature for up to 2 days.

RASPBERRY
ALMOND CHEESECAKE

makes 2 individual-serving cheesecakes

Here, two light cheesecakes are baked over flavorful almond crusts. They're even better the second day, once the flavors have had a chance to mellow and meld. Store the cakes, tightly covered, in the refrigerator overnight—if you can wait that long.

Unsalted butter for greasing the pans
1/4 cup ground toasted almonds
One 8-ounce package cream cheese (regular or low-fat, but not nonfat), at room temperature
1/4 cup sugar
1 medium egg, 2 1/2 tablespoons pasteurized egg substitute such as Egg Beaters, or 5 quail eggs, at room temperature

1 tablespoon sour cream (regular, low-fat, or nonfat)
1 teaspoon all-purpose flour
1/2 teaspoon almond extract
1/4 teaspoon vanilla extract
2 teaspoons raspberry jam
1/8 teaspoon hot water

1. Position the rack in the center of the oven and preheat the oven to 350°F. Generously butter the bottoms and inside walls of two 1 1/2- to 2-cup ramekins, or two 4 1/2-inch springform pans, or two 4-inch paper pastry shells. Spoon 2 tablespoons toasted ground almonds in each pan, then press the ground almonds into the butter on the bottom and sides, forming a crust. Set aside.

2. Beat the cream cheese and sugar in a medium bowl with an electric mixer at medium speed for about 2 minutes, or until light and fluffy. Beat in the egg, egg substitute, or quail eggs for 15 seconds, or until smooth; then beat in the sour cream, flour, almond extract, and vanilla for about 1 minute, until uniform. Divide this mixture between the two prepared pans, gently spooning it into the almond crusts.

3. Whisk the raspberry jam and hot water just until the jam melts. Dot this mixture on top of the cream cheese batter in each pan. Run a knife through the dots, creating swirl patterns in the batter.

4. Bake for 30 minutes, or just until set. Turn off the oven, prop the door open, and leave the cheesecakes in the oven for an additional 30 minutes. Cool completely on a wire rack before unmolding—you may have to run a knife along the inside edges, taking care not to separate the cheesecake from the almond crust. Cover and refrigerate for at least 2 hours, or preferably overnight.

Chocolate Almond Cheesecake

Omit the raspberry jam and water. Instead, melt ½ ounce semisweet chocolate and 1 teaspoon heavy cream in a microwave on high for 1 minute, then continue stirring until the chocolate is melted. Dot this mixture over the cream cheese batter as you did the raspberry jam; drag a knife through the dots to create a chocolate swirl pattern.

BLACK FOREST CAKES 💼

makes 2 individual-serving cakes

Sure, black forest cake is an indulgence: a dense chocolate cake layered with cherries and topped with whipped cream. Here, in a streamlined version for everyday cooking, small, individual chocolate cakes are split open and spread with cherry jam, then topped with sweetened whipped cream. If you want, forgo the cherries and whipped cream and serve the chocolate cakes on their own, with chocolate ice cream perhaps.

1½ tablespoons unsalted butter, plus additional for greasing the pans

¼ cup plus 2 tablespoons all-purpose flour

¼ teaspoon baking powder

¼ teaspoon baking soda

Pinch of salt

¼ cup packed light brown sugar

1½ tablespoons pasteurized egg substitute, such as Egg Beaters; or 3 quail eggs

1 ounce unsweetened chocolate, melted and cooled (see page 17)

¼ teaspoon vanilla extract

¼ cup milk (regular, low-fat, or nonfat)

3 tablespoons cherry jam or preserves

1 cup heavy cream

2 tablespoons granulated sugar

1. Position the rack in the center of the oven and preheat the oven to 350°F. Butter the bottoms and inside walls of two 1½- to 2-cup ramekins, or two 4½-inch springform pans, or two 4-inch paper pastry shells; set aside. Mix the flour, baking powder, baking soda, and salt in a small bowl; set aside.

2. Cream the butter and brown sugar in a medium bowl with a wooden spoon or an electric mixer set at medium speed, beating until the mixture is pale brown and fluffy, about 4 minutes by hand or 2 minutes with the mixer. Beat in the pasteurized egg substitute or quail eggs for 1 minute; then beat in the melted chocolate and vanilla until smooth.

3. Using a wooden spoon, stir one-third of the dry ingredients into the chocolate mixture until moistened; then stir in 2 tablespoons of the milk. Stir in half of the remaining dry ingredients, until moistened; then stir in the remaining 2 tablespoons milk. Finally, stir in the remaining dry ingredients with the wooden spoon, just until incorporated. Do not use an electric mixer or the cake will be tough. Divide the chocolate batter between the prepared pans.

4. Bake for 25 minutes, or until a cake tester or a toothpick comes out clean. Transfer the pans to a wire rack to cool. Cool for 10 minutes in the pans, then unmold and cool completely on the wire rack. If using ramekins, you may need to run a knife around the edge of the cake to loosen it from the sides. If using paper pastry shells, gently tear the shell away from the cake. The cakes can be made in advance; store them, tightly covered, at room temperature for up to 2 days.

5. When the cakes are cooled, use a serrated knife to split them in half so that you create two equal disks. Spread the "bottom" disk of each cake with 1½ tablespoons of the cherry jam or preserves; replace the top disk. In a small chilled bowl, beat the cream until frothy with an electric mixer at medium speed. Turn the mixer to high speed and beat in the granulated sugar, pouring it into the cream in a slow, thin stream. Continue beating until soft peaks form, about 1 minute. Divide this sweetened whipped cream between the two cakes, spooning it onto the tops and spreading it along the sides with a knife. Serve at once.

Cakes and Other Treats

LEMON CAKE
WITH LEMON ICING 📋

makes 2 individual-serving cakes

These light, lemony cakes may be just the sunshine you need in the dead of winter—or any time of year. If you make the cakes in advance, let them stand at room temperature about 1 hour before serving because the icing tastes much better when it's not chilled. For an easier dessert, omit the icing and top the cakes with a scoop of strawberry ice cream.

FOR THE CAKES

2 tablespoons unsalted butter, at room temperature, plus additional for greasing the pans

1/3 cup all-purpose flour, plus additional for dusting the pans

1/4 cup sugar

2 tablespoons pasteurized egg substitute, such as Egg Beaters; or 4 quail eggs

1 1/2 tablespoons milk (regular, low-fat, or nonfat)

1 1/2 teaspoons lemon juice

1/4 teaspoon grated lemon zest

1/4 teaspoon baking powder

1/8 teaspoon baking soda

1/8 teaspoon salt

FOR THE LEMON ICING

2 1/2 tablespoons unsalted butter, at room temperature

3/4 cup (or more) confectioners' sugar

1 tablespoon lemon juice

1/4 teaspoon grated lemon zest

1. To make the cakes, position the rack in the center of the oven and preheat the oven to 350°F. Butter and flour the bottoms and inside walls of two 1 1/2- to 2-cup ramekins, or two 4 1/2-inch springform pans, or two 4-inch paper pastry shells; set aside.

2. Beat the butter and sugar in a medium bowl with a wooden spoon or an electric mixer at medium speed until pale yellow and very fluffy, about 5 minutes by hand or 3 minutes with a mixer. Beat in the pasteurized egg substitute or the quail eggs until smooth, about 1 minute.

3. Using a wooden spoon, stir in the milk, lemon juice, and lemon zest; then stir in the ⅓ cup flour, baking powder, baking soda, and salt, just until barely moistened. Divide this mixture between the prepared pans.

4. Bake for 15 minutes, or until a cake tester or a toothpick comes out clean. Transfer the pans to a wire rack, cool for 10 minutes, then unmold the cakes and cool completely on the wire rack. If using ramekins, you may need to run a knife around the edge of the cake to loosen it from the sides. If using paper pastry shells, gently tear the shell away from the cake. The cakes can be made in advance; store them, tightly covered, at room temperature for up to 2 days.

5. To make the lemon icing, beat the butter with ½ cup of the confectioners' sugar using an electric mixer at medium speed, until smooth and light, about 2 minutes. Beat in the lemon juice and lemon zest, then add another ¼ cup of the confectioners' sugar. Continue beating until smooth, about 1 minute. Beat in more confectioners' sugar if necessary to make a thick, smooth icing, adding it in 1-tablespoon increments.

6. Split the cakes in half so each becomes two equal disks. Frost the bottom layer of each cake with the lemon buttercream, then gently lay the second layer on top. Spoon more of the buttercream over the top, spreading it down the sides of the cake with a knife. Serve immediately, or store, covered, in the refrigerator for up to 1 day.

Cakes and Other Treats

CARROT CAKE WITH
CREAM CHEESE ICING 🍷🍷

makes 2 individual-serving cakes

Make these small, individual versions of the family favorite in advance, if you wish, storing them for up to 2 days, tightly covered, in the refrigerator. The icing, however, is best the minute it's made. Of course, you can forgo the icing and serve the cakes with vanilla frozen yogurt or softened cream cheese.

FOR THE CAKES
Unsalted butter for greasing the pans
½ cup all-purpose flour, plus additional for dusting the pans
¼ teaspoon baking powder
¼ teaspoon baking soda
¼ teaspoon ground cinnamon
⅛ teaspoon of salt
¼ cup plus 2 tablespoons sugar
¼ cup canola oil or other vegetable oil
1 medium egg, at room temperature; or 2½ tablespoons pasteurized egg substitute, such as Egg Beaters; or 5 quail eggs

1 medium carrot, grated (about 6 tablespoons)
1 tablespoon dried currants, or raisins, chopped
1 tablespoon chopped walnuts

FOR THE ICING
2 ounces cream cheese
2 tablespoons unsalted butter, at room temperature
⅛ teaspoon vanilla extract
¼ cup plus 2 tablespoons confectioners' sugar

1. To make the cakes, position the rack in the center of the oven and preheat the oven to 350°F. Butter and flour the bottoms and inside walls of two 1½- to 2-cup ramekins, or two 4½-inch springform pans, or two 4-inch paper pastry shells; set aside. Mix the flour, baking powder, baking soda, cinnamon, and salt in a small bowl; set aside.

2. Beat the sugar and oil in a medium bowl with a wooden spoon or an electric mixer at medium speed until the sugar dissolves and the mixture is smooth, about 3 minutes by hand or 2 minutes with a mixer. Beat in the egg, pasteurized egg substitute, or quail eggs until smooth, or about 1 minute.

3. Using a wooden spoon, stir in the shredded carrots, then the flour mixture, just until incorporated. Stir in the currants and walnuts. Divide this batter between the two prepared pans.

4. Bake for 25 minutes, or until a cake tester or toothpick comes out clean. Transfer the cakes to a wire rack, cool in their pans for 10 minutes, then unmold and cool completely on the wire rack. If using ramekins, you may need to run a knife around the edge of the cake to loosen it from the sides. If using paper pastry shells, gently tear the form away from the cake.

5. To make the icing, beat the cream cheese, butter, and vanilla with an electric mixer at medium speed until light and fluffy. Beat in the confectioners' sugar in 2-tablespoon increments, making sure each has dissolved completely before adding the next. Beat 2 minutes after the final addition, until creamy and smooth. Divide the icing between the two cakes; spoon it onto the top and run it along the sides with a knife. Serve immediately.

Cakes and Other Treats

NUT CAKE

makes **2 individual-serving cakes**

Here, the flour used to make a traditional cake is replaced almost completely with ground nuts. To give the cake some texture and tooth, grind the nuts only until they resemble cornmeal, not dust. The result will be dense, moist, chewy cakes.

2 teaspoons unsalted butter, plus additional for buttering the pans, at room temperature

3 tablespoons sliced almonds

2 tablespoons pecan pieces

2 tablespoons walnut pieces

2 large egg whites, at room temperature

3 tablespoons granulated sugar

1 tablespoon packed light brown sugar

⅛ teaspoon ground cinnamon

⅛ teaspoon of salt

1 large egg yolk, at room temperature

½ teaspoon vanilla extract

1½ tablespoons all-purpose flour

2 tablespoons raspberry jam, or the jam of your choice, or orange marmalade

2 teaspoons confectioners' sugar

1. Position the rack in the center of the oven and preheat the oven to 400°F. Butter the bottoms and sides of two 1½- to 2-cup ramekins, or two 4½-inch springform pans, or two 4-inch paper pastry shells; set aside.

2. Toast all the nuts by placing them in a dry skillet set over medium-low heat for about 4 minutes, or until the nuts are fragrant and lightly browned, stirring frequently. Then grind them in a food processor, a mini food processor, or in a mortar with a pestle; set aside.

3. Beat the egg whites in a large, dry bowl until frothy with an electric mixer at medium speed. Increase the mixer's speed to high and beat until soft, droopy, but moist peaks form, about 2 minutes. Set aside.

4. Mix the granulated sugar, brown sugar, cinnamon, and salt in a medium bowl. Beat in the egg yolk and vanilla with an electric mixer at medium speed until incorporated, about 30 seconds. Then beat in the 2 teaspoons of butter for about 1 minute, until smooth.

5. Using a rubber spatula, stir in the flour and ground nuts. Stir in half the whipped egg whites until smooth; then very gently fold in the remaining egg whites, turning them into the batter. Do not beat or mix vigorously, or the beaten egg whites will not maintain their light airiness. There may be streaks of egg white in the batter. Divide the batter equally between the two prepared pans.

6. Place the pans in the oven and immediately reduce the temperature to 325°F. Bake for 30 minutes, or until a cake tester or toothpick comes out clean. Transfer the cakes to a wire rack and cool for 10 minutes in the pans. Unmold the cakes and cool completely on a wire rack. If using ramekins, you may need to run a knife around the edge of the cake to loosen it from the sides. If using paper pastry shells, gently tear the shell away from the cake.

7. When cooled, split the cakes in half, so that each forms two round disks. Spread 1 tablespoon jam on the "bottom" layer of each cake. Gently press the top layer in place. Serve immediately; or store, covered, at room temperature for up to 1 day. Sift 1 teaspoon confectioners' sugar over each cake just before serving.

Cakes and Other Treats

MOCHA SOUFFLÉS 🧳

makes 2 small soufflés

Soufflés are romantic desserts: light, airy—and they seem as if they should be a lot of trouble. They're not, of course. Prepare these soufflés before dinner, pop them in the oven, and they're done by the time you're ready for dessert. Serve these individual chocolate and coffee soufflés the moment they're done—they deflate once out of the oven.

1 tablespoon unsalted butter, melted and cooled, plus additional for greasing the soufflé dishes and the aluminum foil collars

2½ tablespoons sugar, plus additional for the soufflé dishes

2½ ounces bittersweet or semisweet chocolate, finely chopped

2 tablespoons boiling water

1 teaspoon instant espresso powder (see headnote, page 208)

½ cup milk (regular, low-fat, or nonfat)

1 tablespoon plus 1 teaspoon all-purpose flour

2 large eggs, separated, at room temperature (see Note)

1 teaspoon vanilla extract

⅛ teaspoon of salt

1. Position the rack in the middle of the oven and preheat the oven to 400°F. Butter and sugar two 1½-cup soufflé dishes or high-sided ramekins. Cut two strips of aluminum foil to wrap around the dishes— each strip should be at least 6 inches longer than the circumference of the baking dish, and each should stand up 2 inches above the dish's rim. Butter the shiny sides of the foil pieces. Fold them, butter side in, around the dishes so that the two foil ends meet about 3 inches away from one side of each dish, creating a teardrop shape so that each dish fills out the largest portion of each of the teardrops. Roll and crimp the ends of the aluminum foil together to seal, pressing the crimped ends against the dishes' sides to hold the collar in place. Place the prepared dishes on a baking sheet and set aside.

2. Mix the chocolate, boiling water, and espresso powder in a medium bowl; stir until the chocolate has melted and the espresso powder is dissolved. Set aside for 5 minutes to cool.

3. Meanwhile, whisk the 1 tablespoon melted butter and milk in a large bowl until well combined; then whisk in the flour until incorporated. Whisk in the two egg yolks, the vanilla, and salt, until uniform. Then whisk in the chocolate mixture until smooth. Set aside.

4. Beat the egg whites in a clean, dry medium bowl with an electric mixer at medium speed until frothy, about 30 seconds. Beat in the 2½ tablespoons sugar in a slow, steady stream. Continue beating for about 2 minutes, or until the sugar has dissolved and soft peaks form.

5. Fold the beaten egg whites into the chocolate mixture with a rubber spatula. Take care not to deflate the whites; simply fold them lightly into the chocolate mixture—there will be streaks of egg white visible. Divide this mixture equally between the two prepared soufflé dishes, taking care to spoon it delicately into the dishes without getting it on the foil collars.

6. Bake for 30 minutes, until puffed high. Serve immediately.

> NOTE: The eggs must be separated for this dish—and therein lies the secret to a perfect soufflé. Make sure there is not one speck of yolk in the whites. Let both stand at room temperature for about 20 minutes before proceeding with the recipe. Do not substitute quail eggs or pasteurized egg substitute for the eggs in these soufflés.

ICE CREAM BURRITOS

makes 2 dessert burritos

A sundae wrapped in a flour tortilla? Call it a southwestern twist on the banana split with flavors reminiscent of chocolate pecan turtles.

Two 10- to 12-inch flour
tortillas
2 ounces semisweet chocolate
chips, melted (see
page 17)
¼ teaspoon ground cinnamon

4 small scoops chocolate or
vanilla ice cream
1½ tablespoons jarred caramel
topping, plus additional
caramel topping for garnish
2 tablespoons chopped pecans

1. Place the two tortillas on your work surface. Divide the melted chocolate equally between them, spreading it out with the back of a metal spoon; leave a 1½-inch border all the way around the tortillas. Sprinkle each with ⅛ teaspoon cinnamon.

2. Place two scoops of ice cream in the middle of each tortilla. Divide the caramel topping between the tortillas, drizzling 2 teaspoons over each. Sprinkle each with 1 tablespoon chopped pecans.

3. Fold the burrito closed by bringing the edge nearest you up halfway, then partially cover the ice cream. Fold the sides over to meet in the middle. If they don't meet, just fold them as far as they can go. Fold the "top" down to encase the filling. Turn over so the seams are down, place one ice cream burrito on each of two dessert plates, and serve immediately, garnishing with additional caramel topping, if desired.

Source Guide

Broadway Panhandler
477 Broome Street, New York, NY 10013
1-866-COOKWARE or 1-212-966-3434
www.broadwaypanhandler.com
Springform pans, casseroles, mini food processors, and mandolines

Kalustyan's
123 Lexington Avenue, New York, NY 10016
1-212-685-3451
www.kalustyans.com
An extensive assortment of herbs, oils, and nuts, specializing in
Indian, Middle Eastern, and North African products

Kam Man Food Products
200 Canal Street, New York, NY 10013
1-212-571-0330
A wide assortment of canned, preserved, and dried Chinese and Asian
ingredients

Kitchen Market
218 Eighth Avenue, New York, NY 10011
1-212-243-4433
A great source for most Latin American and Mexican foods, including chiles and spices

Orange Tree Imports
1721 Monroe Street, Madison, WI 53711
1-608-255-8211
www.orangetreeimports.com
A wide selection of cookware and baking tools

Penzeys
P. O. Box 924, Brookfield, WI 53088
1-800-741-7787
www.penzeys.com
A fine purveyor of dried spices and herbs

ThaiGrocer
2961 N. Sheridan Rd., Chicago, IL 60657
1-773-988-8424
www.thaigrocer.com
One of the most complete Thai online grocers

The Wok Shop
718 Grant Avenue, San Francisco, CA 94108
1-888-780-7171
www.wokshop.com
A huge assortment of Asian cooking equipment

www.ultimatecook.com
Extra recipes and information on our other books, all in the Ultimate series: *The Ultimate Ice Cream Book, The Ultimate Party Drink Book, The Ultimate Candy Book, The Ultimate Shrimp Book, The Ultimate Brownie Book,* and *The Ultimate Potato Book*

Index

cumin:
    mayonnaise dressing, 52
    vinaigrette, Southwestern salad
        with chicken, grapefruit and,
        50–52

dill:
    sauce, smoked trout cream cheese
        frittata with, 144–45
    stuffed baked potatoes with
        shrimp, feta and, 88–89
    tabbouleh with shrimp, feta and, 58
duck breasts, pan-seared, with
    honey and figs, 169–70
dumplings, chicken with parsnips,
    leeks and, 158–59

eggplant:
    Parmesan, no-fry, 86–87
    spaghetti with bell pepper, goat
        cheese and, 100–101
eggs, 9, 12
    escarole, white bean and roasted
        garlic soup with, 23
    poached, salad with warm bacon
        dressing and, 46–47
enchiladas, Swiss chard, 119–21
equipment, 5–7
escarole, white bean and roasted
    garlic soup, 22–23

feta cheese:
    in potato spinach casserole,
        84–85
    stuffed baked potatoes with
        shrimp, dill and, 88–89

tabbouleh with shrimp, dill and,
    58
figs, pan-seared duck breasts with
    honey and, 169–70
fish and shellfish, 123–45
    fillets in parchment, 134
    and potato chowder, 30–31
    seafood salad, 56–57
    see also specific fish and shellfish
frittata, smoked trout cream cheese,
    with dill sauce, 144–45
fruit desserts, 237–52
    apple cranberry cobbler, 238–39
    baked bananas with rum, 247
    coconut crepes with tropical fruit
        sauce, 251–52
    ginger honey poached pears,
        248–49
    lemon meringue tartlets, 242–
        43
    rustic apple tart, 240–41
    spiced fruit compote, 250
    strawberry chocolate tartlets,
        245–46
fusilli and meatballs, 98–99

garlic:
    cod roasted over Swiss chard and,
        135–36
    -lemon Cornish game hens,
        163–64
    roasted, escarole and white bean
        soup with, 22–23
    shrimp with peppers and, 124–
        25
gingerbread cookies, 213–14